DEMOCRATIC TRANSITION AND CONSOLIDATION

Jorge I. Domínguez and Anthony Jones, *Series Editors*

DEMOCRACIES IN DANGER

Edited by ALFRED STEPAN

The Johns Hopkins University Press
Baltimore

Printed in the United States of America on acid-free paper

2 4 6 8 9 7 5 3 1

The Johns Hopkins University Press
2715 North Charles Street
Baltimore, Maryland 21218-4363
www.press.jhu.edu

Library of Congress Cataloging-in-Publication Data

Democracies in danger / Alfred Stepan, editor.
p. cm.
Includes bibliographical references and index.
ISBN-13: 978-0-8018-9290-5 (hardcover : alk. paper)
ISBN-10: 0-8018-9290-2 (hardcover : alk. paper)
1. Democracy. 2. Democratization. 3. Political stability.
I. Stepan, Alfred C.
JC423.D38125 2009
321.8—dc22 2008048650

A catalog record for this book is available from the British Library.

Contents

Acknowledgments

The Club of Madrid is an independent organization dedicated to strengthening democracy around the world. The core of its membership is sixty-eight former prime ministers and presidents of new and long-established democracies. Increasingly, the prime ministers and the presidents have involved leading scholars and public and private groups in their general assemblies and in the provision of technical advice and expertise to troubled democracies. I was invited by the president of the Club of Madrid (2003–6), Fernando Henrique Cardoso, to be the academic coordinator of the third general assembly, which involved an intense three-day conversation among the presidents, prime ministers, and academic democracy specialists. All of us who participated in these discussions are grateful that the Club of Madrid was created to respond to the emerging need for addressing the still-intense problems of many new democracies. This volume, like its predecessor *The Construction of Democracy: Lessons from Practice and Research*, edited by Jorge Domínguez and Anthony Jones (Johns Hopkins University Press, 2007), grew out of Club of Madrid debates.

Cardoso, as the former president of Brazil, the former president of the International Sociological Association, and a major activist and theorist of Third Wave democratization efforts, was of course a central figure in the design and execution of the general assembly out of which this volume evolved. Other key planners of the assembly were Kim Campbell, a former prime minister of Canada and the secretary general and vice president of the Club of Madrid, and Jorge Domínguez, Clarence Dillon Professor of International Affairs at Harvard University. Maria Elena Agüero, as director of special projects and institutional relations of the Club of Madrid, was crucial in helping us coordinate all our activities. I am also grateful to Fundación para las Relaciones Internacionales y el Diálogo Exterior (FRIDE), especially its founding president, Diego Hidalgo, and to the Gorbachev Foundation of North America, which created and supported the Club of Madrid and made this book possible. Juan J. Linz and I first started publishing with the Johns Hopkins University Press on democracy in 1978, and, as always, I am grateful for the counsel and encouragement of our editor, Henry Tom.

Democracies in Danger

Introduction

Undertheorized Political Problems in the Founding Democratization Literature

ALFRED STEPAN

Thirty-five years after the Third Wave of democratization began and twenty years after the Berlin Wall came down, many of the new democracies are in danger. There is thus a greater need than ever to think about how they might function better. A group of more than twenty former presidents and prime ministers from Third Wave democracies East and West and a group of invited academics, from many different countries, who specialize in democratization gathered at the third general assembly of the Club of Madrid to address this challenge. The second general assembly had been devoted to domestic and international economic issues, so the planning committee decided to give explicit priority to political issues at the third general assembly.

But what political issues? Given the many urgent politically related problems such as inequality, corruption, new forms of authoritarian populism, decline of trust, the weakness of programmatic parties, narco-trafficking, and terrorism that were putting many of the new democracies in danger, there was potentially a huge and unmanageable agenda for a three-day meeting. We thus made two more planning decisions. The first decision was to focus on only three issues so that in the course of the assembly we could have a reasonable amount of time for the activists and theorists to *diagnose* the origins of the problem and attempt to evaluate possible *prescriptions*. The second planning decision was that, given the plethora of potential problems, we should privilege issues that the first generation of democratization theorists had dangerously neglected or, if we had not neglected, on which we now felt we had been wrong or where new research was beginning to suggest political reforms or experiments of the sort not considered in the foundational literature.

These decisions eliminated some candidate problems such as inequality, not because inequality is not an urgent problem but because the foundational literature had addressed it, and the original diagnosis and prescription of the need for enhanced high-quality educational opportunities, greater citizen access to power, and better patterns of income maintenance and distribution is still consensual. In contrast, there were some issues that had indeed been almost completely neglected by the first generation of the democratization literature. For example, not one chapter in the four-volume series, *Transitions from Authoritarian Rule,* which did more than any other work to establish the field of democratic transition studies (to which I contributed and thus share the blame), is devoted to ethnic and religious conflicts and/or wars of secession of the sort that destroyed Yugoslavia, are threatening the chances of democracy in Nigeria, and are shattering the onetime most peaceful and successful model of democracy in South Asia, Sri Lanka.[1] And, of course, given our focus on transitions in southern Europe and South America, we were silent on the issue of Islam and democracy. Given our previous neglect of possible ways to manage ethnic and religious conflicts peacefully and democratically, these challenges had to be debated at our third general assembly.

We, the first generation of democratization theorists, also virtually did not ask the question of how the new democracies would democratically manage their security apparatuses—the military, police, and intelligence services. Almost all our attention had been devoted to how to get rid of the old authoritarian, often military, regimes, but collectively we did not write much about how the military should be reconfigured. On how the police could be transformed from a threat to citizens and a source of corruption to a critical resource to enhance citizens' security we had been nearly silent. Nor had we addressed how democracies could create new and efficacious intelligence systems *within* and *between* all democracies to deal with global networks of narco-trafficking and terrorism without diminishing newly won liberties of citizens. More than any other first-generation democratization theorist, I am aware of, and responsible for, these lacunae because I wrote the most about security issues between 1971 and 1986. In my three books on security, I devoted only one chapter to how democratic citizens and leaders could manage their military, police, and intelligence services. Fortunately this present volume gives us the opportunity to identify recent pioneering research and to evaluate newly emerging "best practices" in this critical area that we had not only under-theorized but almost completely ignored.

A third major corrective opportunity also appeared to us. The first generation of democratization theorists did not neglect the analysis of the forms of democratic executives. For example, we produced a substantial literature on the relative merits of presidentialism versus parliamentarianism, especially as to whether they were "military-coup inducing" or "military-coup inhibiting." And when possible changes away from presidentialism were considered in countries such as Brazil, Argentina, and even Chile, the implicit model was toward a rather unexamined, and we now believe profoundly misconceptualized, French-style parliamentarism normally called semi-presidentialism. However, our political and theoretical debates devoted almost no attention to possible new variants of presidentialism or semi-presidentialism. We therefore decided that in our upcoming general assembly, academics and political leaders alike should discuss as their third question whether we could begin to think of promising new variants of democratic executive power.

Fortunately we were able to commission two writers for each of these three questions. They wrote background papers that were discussed by former prime ministers and presidents and then rewritten for this volume. We attacked our three questions in the following ways.

HOW TO MANAGE POTENTIAL CULTURAL CONFLICTS PEACEFULLY, DEMOCRATICALLY, AND SUCCESSFULLY

While cultural conflicts over nationalism, religion, language, and race were, as I have stressed, badly neglected in the classic foundational studies of democratization, they obviously are of intense concern now in many new democracies. Given the growing salience of "uncivil societies," we particularly wanted to re-explore our original ideas about "civil society," which was the "celebrity" of transitions in countries such as Brazil and Poland, and give more attention to what actually makes a cooperative, as opposed to a conflictual, civil society.

These issues are addressed in a chapter on ethno-communal-religious riots and varieties of civil society by Ashutosh Varshney and a chapter on the democratic and peaceful management of secessionist demands by Richard Simeon.

In my view, three key steps in recent theorizing about civil society are relevant to our concerns in this volume. The first step is associated with Robert Putnam and is widely followed in thinking about new democracies. A core theme of Putnam is that the greater the density and activity of civil society, the better it is for democracy.[2] The second major step was taken by Sheri Berman when she noted that in the 1920s, one of the countries most similar to the United States in terms of density and robustness of civil society was Weimar Germany.[3] Her devastating point of course is that we have to not only think about density, but about the political content and context of different types of activities in civil society, and whether they help or hurt democratic life in the polis. The third major step was taken by the Indian social scientist, Ashutosh Varshney. In a prize-winning book about India, Varshney identified and explained why some types of civil society formations (especially those that combined Muslims and Hindus together in activities aimed at producing communal peace) were in fact "riot-inhibiting", whereas equally dense civil society groupings of Muslims only, or Hindus only, were often "riot-inducing."[4]

Varshney is now engaged in a major extension of his original research by broad-ranging fieldwork in some important Muslim majority states: Indonesia, which is now a democracy; Nigeria, which for a time was a borderline democracy with substantial communal conflict; and Malaysia, which has managed ethnic conflict reasonably well but is not yet a democracy with fully fair and free elections. In this volume Varshney discusses for the first time some of the results from his new research. His interim data show that, with some important conceptual and political refinements of his classic Indian study, the core argument about riot-inhibiting and riot-inducing types of civil society organizations holds.[5]

Finally, much of the civil society literature assumes that civil society must be independent of the state. However, Varshney shows how some "riot-inhibiting" civil society groups were helped in their formation by state actors. He then explores what this means for civil society theory and for acceptable democratic practices.

Our second article, by the eminent Canadian scholar of comparative federalism, Richard Simeon, focuses on the question of secession. Often ethno-secessionist movements, such as those in the Balkans, Nigeria, Sri Lanka, and Chechnya, have been marked by hatreds, numerous killings by all sides, and authoritarian practices. Many observers thus see all secessionist movements as democratic failures and secession to be avoided at all costs.

Nonetheless, in numerous parts of the world, secessionist demands continue to figure prominently. Despite this fact, democratization leaders have not worked sufficiently on identifying a set of practices and democratization theorists have not developed a body of literature devoted to how secession struggles, whatever the outcome, can possibly be conducted peacefully and democratically. Simeon addresses these critical issues in his discussion of Quebec. My reading of Simeon's article left me thinking that even if Quebec were to become an independent state, the political process of secession management would be a success because there would be no violence, both independent Quebec and independent Canada would remain consolidated democracies, and the social and economic systems of neither country would be seriously disrupted.

Simeon's rich analysis of the complex reasons for these probable outcomes directs our attention to a number of key factors: the evolution of Canada's de facto "asymmetrical federalism"; the construction of "civic nationalism," especially since the 1960s, in *all* parts of Canada; the collective "saying of no to violence" that emerged when the first and only political killing related to secession was committed in 1970; and the critical role of a neutral state institution, the Canadian Supreme Court, especially in their 1998 decision, that said that if there were referendum with a "clear question" and a "clear result" favoring Quebec's secession, the rest of Canada would have a "constitutional obligation" to negotiate the matter.

HOW TO CREATE AND CONTROL DEMOCRATICALLY USABLE HUMAN SECURITY SERVICES

Most participants at our assembly, both political leaders and democratization theorists, came of age in a world where many nondemocratic regimes fused military, police, and intelligence services. Much of the original thinking about democratic transitions was understandably focused on getting rid of these fused and dictatorial structures.

But the focus was on opposition. Most of the theoretical reflection was on civil society, not enough on political society, and very little about what to do with the coercive apparatus of the state if and when democrats came to power.[6]

Citizens have inalienable rights, but if there is no usable state with a democratically controlled coercive apparatus, citizens' rights cannot be effectively defended in a new democracy. To the extent that democratic leaders had a policy toward the security apparatus at the start of the transition, it was focused on getting the old incumbents out of power (even if most missions and prerogatives were left intact) and then to divide the control of the military, police, and intelligence as much as possible. But few democratic leaders or thinkers had a strategy for rebuilding their security apparatus.

Now, thirty-five years after the third democratic wave began, many countries are experiencing declining support for democracy because the citizens feel they have no accessible and effective state in the area of the police.

In countries where globally coordinated terrorism and/or narco-trafficking are lowering the quality of life in democracies, and in some cases threatening the institutions of democracy themselves, it is also increasingly clear that the old model of each country acting autonomously and domestically separating intelligence, police, and the armed forces is no longer adequate.

Many of the former presidents and prime ministers at the general assembly were certain that there had to be increasing national and international coordination of police, intelligence, and military operations to protect democracies.[7] However, they were equally worried about how to avoid the erosion—of the sort many saw occurring in Guantánamo—of traditional democratic legal norms. Thus, the second major theme of the book is how to create and control democratically usable human security services.

Many new endangered democracies face what the Chile-born scholar Felipe Agüero calls in his article, "The New 'Double Challenge': Simultaneously Crafting Democratic Control and Efficacy Concerning Military, Police, and Intelligence." Successfully confronting this new double challenge of control *and* efficacy will require completely new types of policy and academic specialists and a virtually new literature that we must rapidly incorporate into comparative democratization studies. Agüero's richly referenced article is a beginning of such a new literature.

Agüero's arguments are multiple and compounding. There needs to be a significant shift away from the ideology of and training for "national territorial security" to training for "citizens' human security."[8] The promotion of citizens' human security must involve an integrated approach to good democratic governance within the state as well as within the police, intelligence, and armed forces. This new approach is beginning to be called "security sector reform."[9] Agüero, who is a member of the International Advisory Board of the Global Facilitation Network for Security Sector Reform, analyzes some of the successes associated with this new approach. The foundational studies of democratization placed emphasis on the "sequencing" of reforms; however, human security sector reforms must to some extent be addressed simultaneously. For example, in most of the new democracies that had been immediately preceded by military rule, almost all the initial reform efforts were devoted to military issues and neglected the police. But this experience has now clearly shown that such sequencing produces its own problems. A "weak or ineffective police will put pressure on officials to use the military for public order duties" or to militarize the police. He argues that the primary reason for the disappointing progress in reforms is due, not so much to resistance by the security services, but the "inaction, complicit stance, or active encouragement of nondemocratic behavior by civilian actors in government or political society."

Agüero's last point brings us to the key role of democratic leadership concerning security sector reform. In many specialists' judgment, the most imaginative and effective minister of defense of any Third Wave democracy was Narcís Serra of Spain. A civilian, academic, and former mayor of Barcelona, he served as minister of defense from 1982 to 1990 and carried out reforms in virtually every aspect of civil-military relations. Serra's democratic civilian leadership is precisely the sort that Agüero is urging. It is thus an important event that for this volume Serra presents his first major publication in English, in which he spells out the key principles he followed and how he designed and implemented his reforms. Serra is also considered in Europe as a key thinker and activist concerning new democratic policies against terrorism. At my and Fernando Henrique Cardoso's urging, he discusses some of Europe's new policy approaches to these challenges.

Serra begins by spelling out the key tasks that he, working with the democratic government and legislature, had to carry out before he considered the democratic *transition* to be completed in the area of the armed forces. First was removing the military from their full involvement in political power. The second task was striving to almost completely reduce the military's *de facto* tutelage of the new democratizing government, a tutelage stemming from the military's view of themselves as still the guardians of the nation and able to act unilaterally if they deemed the situation so required. And the third task was eliminating the military's "conditioning" of policies of elected governments, due to the military's capacity to limit the reach, or even to veto, some crucial reforms.

Serra then goes on to spell out the additional tasks that he and the new democracy had to complete before the democratic regime could be *consolidated.* His first posttransition task was to eliminate the military's organizational and political autonomy in terms of budget control, definition of mission, and force structure. He believes that this can only be done if civilian democratic leadership, and especially the ministry of defense, is able to develop, articulate, and lead a credible alternative military policy. The second task was the winning of military acceptance of democratic civilian and judicial supremacy. His third task was to get ideological and educational control of the military as a whole. Serra argues that it took thirteen years, 1975–88, to achieve all six of these pre- and posttransition tasks in Spain.

One of the great virtues of Serra's discussion of these six tasks is that their clear enumeration allows citizens in any new democracy to conduct an inventory of how far their country has come, or not come, towards consolidating democratic control of the military. In my judgment some new democracies have only carried out the first task, others three or four, but very few have yet to complete all six.

The final part of Serra's article is his analysis of military, police, and intelligence reforms needed in both new (and old) democracies in response to transnational terrorism and narco-trafficking. He argues that the most dangerous combination most new democracies face is the fusion of these three services under military control. He thus urges an initial decentralization of the services under democratic control. But then, no doubt to the surprise of some readers, he advocates a careful crafting of some recentralized national and international capacities, such as intelligence sharing, new and coordinated transnational legal codes that facilitate rapid extradition within democracies, and police who see protecting citizens' security as their first priority.

Serra is aware that there is the danger of recreating excessive and autonomous power, even though it is now in the hands of a democratic executive. He thus recommends a variety of reforms to protect citizens' rights and to control the democratic executive, such as an enhanced role for an independent judiciary, autonomous intelligence review boards, and reinvigorated legislative capabilities.

NEW PROPOSALS ON HOW TO REFINE PRESIDENTIALISM AND SEMI-PRESIDENTIALISM

The fundamental models (each with many variants) of democratic governance among the world's modern democracies are parliamentarianism (as first founded in the United Kingdom), semi-presidentialism (as exemplified by the French Fifth Republic), and presidentialism (as first founded in the United States of America).[10] At our discussions at the Club of Madrid, there emerged a consensus that many of the democracies currently in danger were so in part because of tendencies within the models of presidentialism and semi-presidentialism that had not been analyzed adequately at the start of the new wave of democratization.

To be sure, many democratic activists and democratic theorists, concerned about some of the rigidities of presidentialism as a system, had discussed the possibility of a full-scale substitution of presidentialism by parliamentarianism. But efforts to replace or reform presidentialism waned after the mid-1990s for two main reasons.

First, in one democracy after another, democratic politicians and democratic voters could not bring themselves to back away from the chance of having a powerful, democratically elected president, who they believed could push the reforms most citizens wanted. Whatever the weight of the theoretical arguments against presidentialism, the political struggle against presidentialism seemed unwinnable.

Second, one of the most politically powerful arguments against presidentialism seemed to be challenged by historical events. Critics had argued that presidentialism contributed to coups and military governments. Indeed, in the 1960s and 1970s only five of the twenty countries in Latin America avoided military regimes. But, from the 1990s until today, military regimes have been disappearing in new democracies of East Asia and Latin America. Indeed, in 2009, there is not one military regime in Latin America.

But, as Arturo Valenzuela argues in this volume, some new and disturbing trends related to presidentialism in Latin America suggest that once again we need to rethink how the institutions of presidentialism, especially their Latin American variants, could be fundamentally reformed.

There may be no military regimes at the moment in Latin America, but as Valenzuela documents, since 1983 *sixteen* presidents have been forced out of office before their constitutional terms had expired, a seventeenth president interrupted the constitutional order by closing congress, and many others have only been able to pass legislation by decree. Today, among the world's democracies, many of the lowest chief-executive approval ratings and much of the weakest legislative support and highest public-opinion support for nondemocratic alternatives to carry out changes are found in gridlocked Latin American presidential democracies. So there is a *new crisis of democratic efficacy and democratic legitimacy* in Latin America, and Valenzuela marshals powerful evidence to show that much of this crisis is related to presidentialism.

However, alternatives to strengthen such presidential democracies in danger have begun to emerge from years of discussions of Valenzuela with the great Argentine legal theorist, Carlos Nino, the seminal theorist of democracy, Juan Linz, and the beleaguered and eventually overthrown Bolivian president, Gonzalo Sánchez de Lozada. I call these alternatives "parliamentarized presidentialism." Given the numerous crises of presidentialism, the Club of Madrid as a group, and I as the editor, convinced Valenzuela of the need to debate these alternatives within our general assembly and eventually to make some of them available in print for the first time in this volume.

I participated in numerous discussions in Brazil, Chile, and Argentina in the 1980s and early 1990s about the desirability and feasibility of substituting presidentialism with a form of parliamentarianism. With few exceptions, the form of parliamentarianism that was most desired by political leaders and the public was actually French-style semi-presidentialism, because it entailed a dual executive with a prime minister responsible to parliament, but it still had a directly elected president.[11] In retrospect, it is fascinating how little attention we actually devoted to an exploration of possible problems with semi-presidentialism.

Cindy Skach, the author of a major book on semi-presidentialism, and Timothy J. Colton, one of the leading scholars on Russian politics, have teamed up in this volume to give us the critical assessment of the theory and practice of semi-presidentialism that we lacked at the beginning of the Third Wave.[12] They do this by comparing the postcommunist experience, particularly in Russia, with the French Fifth Republic, and with the neglected but increasingly attractive model of Portugal. They have a new rich body of empirical evidence to examine because semi-presidentialism became the modal form of governance adopted in postcommunist Europe.[13] They use this body of evidence to show that there is much more variation, and potential dangers for democracy within some of these variations, than had previously been diagnosed.

As they point out, most analyses of semi-presidentialism discuss two electorally produced forms of the model's intrinsic "dual executive." Position one: the president is a leader of a party or a coalition with a majority in both houses. Position two: the president does not have a majority in the parliament, but the prime minister does.[14]

One of the reasons some people argued that semi-presidentialism was the best of both worlds was that they saw what I call position one as pure presidentialism with a legislative majority, and considered it to be thus exempt from the problems of divided government. They saw position two as close to pure parliamentarianism, because there is a prime minister who governs with a legislative majority and is the leader of the government. Thus, for some writers, such as Arend Lijphart, there is no dangerous space in semi-presidentialism (which almost does not exist as a separate form of governance) because it really only involves an *alternation* (from position one to position two and back) between the two least problematic forms of presidentialism or parliamentarianism.

However, there are indeed problematic spaces in semi-presidentialism. Position two is never actually close to pure parliamentarianism. The head of state is a directly elected president with a fixed term, and the presidential office often has constitutionally embedded prerogatives concerning external and internal security, intelligence, foreign affairs, emergency and decree powers, and the right to dissolve parliament and call for new elections. This is *not* pure parliamentarianism but a "dual executive," with two different electoral sources of legitimacy. The office of a directly elected president in semi-presidentialism with these powers thus has a firmer base within the state to contest the prime minister than any office could possibly have in pure parliamentarianism.

But I have not discussed the most problematic space of semi-presidentialism. Positions one and two do not in fact exhaust the electorally produced possibilities of the model. Logically, there can be a position three, where *neither* the president *nor* the prime minister has a majority.[15]

The potential problems of position three were neglected in the foundational literature of democratization studies because it was not sufficiently recognized as a possibility. The major model most democratic activists and theorists had in mind, the French Fifth Republic, was for its first twenty-six years always in position one and had *never* been in position three.[16] However, as Colton and Skach argue, many of the new semi-presidential countries such as Russia have almost *always* been in position three.

They argue that position three is the most fraught with dangers for democracy because both the dual executives, even though neither has a legislative majority, have some constitutional claims to executive prerogatives. They argue that position three situations are often resolved by presidents using their constitutionally embedded emergency powers and special access to intelligence, police, and military resources to alter the balance of forces by nondemocratic measures.

Colton and Skach demonstrate in telling detail how, in the Russian case, position three contributed to President Yeltsin often ruling on the margins of democracy or temporarily going "out of the democratic box," as in 1993, by closing the parliament by force, creating a new "super-presidential" constitution while parliament was closed, and then getting that constitution ratified under plebiscitary circumstances.

What emerges from Colton and Skach's analysis is that we need to be aware not only of French-style Fifth Republic semi-presidentialism (which in my judgment is now empirically a cell of one) but of two much more prominent patterns, Yeltsin-like "super-presidential semi-presidentialism" and the emerging pattern that I call "parliamentarized semi-presidentialism." This last pattern of politics and executive party constitutional relations is virtually unstudied. It developed first in Portugal and, with variants, is now predominant in Poland, Slovenia, Lithuania, and Croatia.

By the phrase "parliamentarized semi-presidentialism," I mean to call attention to a conscious set of political decisions and actions that might be deliberately taken by leaders, constitutional designers, and voters in order to reduce some potential problems with semi-presidentialism. The proposal entails a directly elected president, but, as in Portugal, Poland, Lithuania, Slovenia, and most recently Croatia, there is the deliberate effort to avoid "super-presidentialism" by reducing the powers of the president and increasing the powers of the parliament and often the courts.[17] The effect of these changes is to increase incentives for elected politicians and prime ministers to build and sustain democratic parties and coalitions. This is so because, in this form of semi-presidentialism, aspirant political leaders cannot lead the democratic government if the majority of parliament is against them.

In my judgment this form of semi-presidentialism will be the least dangerous to democracy because it will make position three much less likely to occur. Furthermore, while it would not eliminate the tensions between the dual executives endemic to position two, it would render them less dangerous—the president has fewer powers in Slovenia and Lithuania than in France, and Portugal and Poland are now considered relatively weak presidencies.[18]

A look at the eight postcommunist countries admitted into the European Union in 2004, and therefore deemed to have passed an important threshold of democratic consolidation, is extremely illustrative. Five of the new member countries are pure parliamentary—Hungary, the Czech Republic, Estonia, Latvia, and Slovakia. None were French-style Fifth Republic semi-presidential. None were "super-presidential semi-presidential." All of the remaining three new European Union members—Poland, Slovenia, and Lithuania—are close to "parliamentarized semi-presidentialism."

The value of identifying this new pattern is not only that it calls attention to these new *political arrangements* as such but also that it alerts us to an unexpected, and democratically usable, political *process*. It suggests that there are types of actions that can be taken by democratic leaders and voters to mitigate some of the dangers to democracy of semi-presidential rule.

The volume ends with a conclusion by one of the most influential intellectual leaders of the first generation of democratization theorists, Fernando Henrique Cardoso, who also became an efficacious pioneer of second-generation democratic reforms during his two terms as president of Brazil, from 1995 to 2003.

PART ONE

Managing Potential Cultural Conflicts Democratically

CHAPTER ONE

Civil Society, Islam, and Ethnocommunal Conflict

ASHUTOSH VARSHNEY

Some other contributions in this volume focus on national-level political institutions, such as "asymmetric federalism." Drawing upon my research in India, Indonesia, Malaysia, and Sri Lanka, I will focus on civil society, defined as the non-state sphere of our collective life, in which organizations relatively independent of the state exist and function.[1] I do so to address the question of why ethnocommunal conflicts have been endemic in the world and to ask what kinds of civil society associations might inhibit outbreaks of such conflicts. As is well known, such conflicts have a negative impact on the quality, and sometimes the survival, of democracy. This new research presents a fresh diagnosis of ethnocommunal violence.

Where necessary, I will also make brief remarks on the relationship between Islam and conflict. In the current intellectual and political climate, a great deal of attention is being paid to the role of Islam in politics. Muslims are in a majority in two of the countries mentioned above—Indonesia and Malaysia—and a minority in India and Sri Lanka. India is among the oldest and most stable democracies in the developing world; Indonesia has been a functioning democracy since 1998; Malaysia is normally viewed as a semi-democracy; and Sri Lanka was a democracy for three decades before unchecked majoritarianism undermined its democratic vibrancy in 1983 and led to a civil war. At this point, Sri Lanka is at best a semi-democracy: there is vigorous contestation between the two main political parties for the vote of the majority community, but the electoral participation of the principal minority community, the Tamils, is minimal (though the same cannot be said of other minority communities, especially the Moors). It is possible to develop some ideas, based on the experiences of these countries, about the role Islam plays in ethnocommunal conflict, especially in democratic or semi-democratic settings.

I shall present two kinds of conclusions toward the end of this essay: one about how civil society can moderate ethnic violence, and another about how the link between Islam and violence, often assumed to be axiomatic these days, is mediated, among other things, by the local relationships into which Muslim communities may be interwoven with others. The argument that violence is inherent to Islam is not sustainable.

CLARIFYING TERMS

To avoid possible confusion, two terms should first be clearly defined: civil society and ethnocommunal conflict. Different scholars understand the terms differently. How do I interpret them?

By civil society, I mean that space in our social life that is located between the state institutions on the one hand and families on the other, that allows people voluntarily to come together for a whole variety of public activities, and that is relatively independent of the state. Civil society is not a *nonpolitical* but a *non-state* space of collective life. Moreover, in its non-state functions, it can embrace both social and political activities. Soccer leagues, playing-card societies, and philately, music, and film clubs may be social, not political; but trade unions and political parties in multiparty systems (not in single-party systems) are primarily the latter, not the former, though in the process of playing their political roles, they may also provide social platforms for coming together.[2] Both types of organizations are parts of civil society, so long as they are independent of the state.

Are "ethnocommunal conflict" and "ethnocommunal violence" the same, or should we draw a distinction between the two? On the whole, most of the existing literature has not distinguished ethnocommunal violence from ethnocommunal conflict. In any ethnically and religiously plural society, where freedom of expression is available, some ethnocommunal conflict is more or less inevitable.

The key issue is whether ethnocommunal conflict (ethnic or communal conflict henceforth) is violent, or nonviolent, and waged in the institutionalized channels of the polity. If ethnic grievances are expressed in the recognized institutions of the polity—in parliaments, in assemblies, in bureaucracies—and ameliorative action is sought there, or alternatively, if it takes the form of nonviolent demonstrations on the streets, civil disobedience being the zenith of such politics, it is conflict to be sure, but not violence. Such institutionalized conflict, which can be quite healthy for a polity in many ways, must not be equated with a situation in which protest becomes violent, riots take place, pogroms are initiated against some ethnic groups with connivance of state authorities, and, in its most extreme form, a civil war breaks out. Ethnocommunal peace should, for all practical purposes, be conceptualized as an institutionalized channeling and resolution of ethnic conflicts. It should be visualized as an absence of *violence*, not as an absence of *conflict*. We might perhaps live in a more peaceful world if we could eliminate ethnic and national conflicts from our midst, but a post-ethnic, post-national era does not seem be in the offing, at least in the short to medium run.

THE PUZZLE

Sooner or later, a puzzling empirical regularity confronts scholars of ethnic conflict. Despite ethnic diversity, some places—nations, regions, towns, villages—remain peaceful, whereas others with the same diversity experience frequent outbursts of violence. Similarly, some multiethnic societies, after maintaining a long record of peace, explode all of a sudden. Variations across time and space have until recently not been a focus of inquiry in the field of ethnicity and nationalism. My book, *Ethnic Conflict and Civic Life*, dealt with variation across space; a new project, described later, deals primarily with variations across time.

To understand variations across space on Hindu-Muslim violence in India, my book examined all reported Hindu-Muslim riots in the country between 1950 and 1995.[3] Two results were crucial. First, the share of villages involved in communal rioting was remarkably small. Rural India, where two out of three Indians still live, accounted for a mere 3.6 percent of all deaths in communal violence in this period. Hindu-Muslim violence is primarily an urban phenomenon. Secondly, within urban India, Hindu-Muslim riots were highly locally concentrated. Eight cities—Ahmedabad, Bombay, Aligarh, Hyderabad, Meerut, Baroda, Calcutta, and Delhi—accounted for a hugely disproportionate share of communal violence in the country: roughly half of all urban deaths and 45 percent of all deaths in communual violence, urban as well as rural. As a group, however, these eight cities represent less than a fifth of India's urban population (and only about 5–6 percent of the country's total population). Eighty-two percent of the urban population has not been "riot-prone."

In other words, India's Hindu-Muslim violence is city-specific. State (and national) politics is best seen as providing the context within which the local mechanisms linked with violence, or peace, get activated. To explain communal violence, we must thoroughly investigate these local mechanisms.

Are these patterns by any chance specific only to India? While in-country patterns of rioting have not been systematically investigated for many countries, what we do know suggests that Indian patterns are not peculiar. In Indonesia, a mere fifteen districts (*kabupaten*), holding 6.5 percent of the country's total population, accounted for 85.5 percent of all deaths in group violence short of civil wars between 1990 and 2003.[4] The data that we have on racial violence in the United States in the twentieth century and on Northern Ireland's "disturbances" since the late 1960s also show roughly similar larger patterns.[5]

Ethnocommunal violence tends to be highly *locally or regionally concentrated*, not evenly geographically spread in a country. Before ethnic conflicts become civil wars, a countrywide breakdown of ethnic relations is rare. We tend to form partial, or wrong, impressions of ethnic violence, because violence is what attracts the attention of media, not the quiet continuation of routine life, or because we derive conclusions about ethnic conflict in general from *civil wars* that are, however, only one, though the deadliest, type of ethnic conflict. A lot of ethnic violence takes the form of *riots* before civil wars break out, and short of civil wars, it is more common to have pockets of violence surrounded by vast stretches of peace.

The principal difference between riots and civil wars is simply that even as the state's neutrality may be in doubt during riots, the state does not suspend the principle of neutrality, nor does it become a combatant in ethnic strife. During civil wars, the state drops the principle of neutrality altogether and also becomes a combatant against a group challenging the state. Riots and civil wars are thus very different phenomena.

THE DOMINANT EXPLANATORY TRADITIONS

Until recently, scholars had four major explanations for ethnocommunal violence. By the recent standards of scholarship, these explanations suffer from several deficiencies, which I will briefly discuss at the end of this section. The most important gap for my purposes here is the incapability of these traditions to explain local concentrations of ethnocommunal violence, the key empirical finding reported above. Let us look at each tradition in turn.

The first major explanation, by far the most popular in the journalistic and popular circles, is also known as "primordialism."[6] It refers to "primordial or ancient animosities" as a cause of contemporary conflict. The animosities, lasting for centuries, are said to be based on differences of race, religion, or culture. Conflicts result, for a rational calculus is overtaken by the emotional ties of blood or by ancient hatreds. Though this view is popular in journalism, few scholars today subscribe to the idea of ancient animosities. To put it simply, they believe that most ethnic conflicts, if not religious ones, are modern or that, even if one finds evidence of their prevalence in premodern times, the meaning and scale of those conflicts were very different. Modernity has not led to the disappearance of ethnic or religious identities, as was widely assumed by scholars, intellectuals, and politicians after the Second World War. Rather, it can be shown that for a whole variety of reasons, modernity can activate ethnic or religious conflict.

The second big tradition is known as "instrumentalism." Its key proposition is that ancient animosities are not the main issue; rather, the political elite uses ethnicity for political or economic purposes, regardless of whether the elite believes in ethnicity. Conflicts are a result of such cynical instrumental manipulation. This view has not been able to resolve a major puzzle: the elite may indeed gain power by mobilizing ethnic identity, without actually believing in it, but why should the masses follow the leaders, especially if the costs of participation are known to be high and may include imprisonment, injury, or death?[7]

The third tradition, more recent than the previous two, has come to be called "constructivism." The principal proposition of constructivists is that our contemporary identities as Hindus or Muslims, as Jews or Christians, as Tibetans or Han Chinese are *modern*, not ancient. The claim is not that there were no Hindus, Muslims, Jews, Christians, Tibetans, and Han Chinese in premodern times. Rather, identities in premodern times tended on the whole to be face-to-face and operated on a small scale. Ordinary people rarely interacted beyond their local environments. Conflict, when it emerged, was managed locally, and identities were considerably flexible. Extra-local communities did not include "the people"; such larger communities consisted primarily of the ecclesiastical elite and the court-based aristocracy and nobility.[8] Modernity changed the meaning of identities by bringing the masses into a larger, extra-local, framework of consciousness. It made identities and communities broader and more institutionalized. In what has become a classic constructivist argument, Linda Colley shows how shared Protestantism, opposition to France, and the benefits of empire managed to dissolve the bitter historical disputes between the Scots and the English and led to the construction of a British identity in the eighteenth and nineteenth centuries.[9] And in Benedict Anderson's *Imagined Communities*, one of the most influential texts on nationalism today, the emphasis is on how modern technology and a modern economic system—the printing press and capitalism, to be more precise—made it possible to have imaginations about large and popular communities, which overtook the premodern, extra-local, religious communities of the clergymen on the one hand and the aristocratic dynasties on the other.

The fourth big tradition goes by the name of "institutionalism." Its central idea is that there are clearly identifiable connections between ethnic conflict (or peace) on the one hand and political institutions on the other. It matters whether multiethnic societies have consociational or majoritarian democracies, federal or unitary governments, single- or multimember constituencies, proportional representation versus a first-past-the-post electoral system. Ethnic pluralism, it is argued, requires political institutions—forms and rules of power sharing, types of constituencies, varieties of voting systems, party systems—different from those that are appropriate for ethnically homogeneous, or at any rate, ethnically undivided, societies. An uncritical adoption of institutional forms, regardless of whether a society is marked by ethnic divisions, can be a serious cause of ethnic conflict. An institutional choice suited to the ethnic map of a society resolves, or at any rate mitigates, conflict.

Three major deficiencies of this literature, two conceptual, one empirical, are worthy of our attention.[10] The conceptual deficiencies have to do with two new ideas —mechanisms and variations—that have driven the evolution of research in the last ten years.

In earlier times, scholars often used to leave theory building to a link between structural conditions and the rise of ethnic conflict or nationalism. Ernest Gellner is the best-known example of this tendency.[11] He argued that the rise of industrial age required nationalism, as linguistic standardization became necessary for communication between citizens, and the rural masses moved to cities in search of industrial employment. Given the social science norms of the 1990s, this sort of reasoning is no longer viewed as sufficiently rigorous. The fact that industrialization *requires* nationalism does not mean that it would happen. Can need create its own fulfillment? Many needs go unrealized in history and politics. At the very least, an account of the organizations, movements, or leaders that would undertake the task of converting needs into actual outcomes is required.

The idea of variance, similarly, has made advances possible. Theorizing about ethnic violence used to be based on establishing commonalities across the many cases of violence (or sometimes based on an in-depth case study or two).[12] By the mid-1990s, following the popularity of King, Keohane, and Verba, this came to be called "selection bias" and was deemed inadmissible for derivation of causality.[13]

Selection bias, it was later noted, was not entirely useless. It could, for example, undermine an existing theory, if the generalizations based on similar cases led to an argument opposed to the existing theoretical orthodoxy.[14] But in and of its own, it was not enough to generate a new, empirically valid, causal theory.

However, given the purposes of this essay, the most important gap of the traditional literature lies elsewhere. These theories are unable to account for the local/geographical concentrations of ethnic violence. If the primordial, instrumental, and constructivist arguments, all pitched at a very general level, were true, why would there be such variations *within* countries? If national political institutions were decisive, why would there be *intranational* differences? Clearly, something locally specific is also involved which, when discovered and included, begins to explain variations with or without national-level explanations.

DISCOVERING THE ROLE OF CIVIL SOCIETY

Following this reasoning, my book on India selected six cities—three riot-prone and three peaceful—and arranged them in three pairs. Each pair contained a city where communal violence was endemic and a city where it was rare or entirely absent. To ensure that we did not compare apples and oranges, roughly similar percentages of Hindus and Muslims in the city populations constituted the minimum control in each pair.[15]

The relationship between civil society and ethnocommunal violence emerged from this comparison. To be more specific, my argument was focused on the *inter*communal links (networks and organizations that integrate Hindus and Muslims), not *intra*communal links (networks and organizations that are all Hindu or all Muslim). In an evocative turn of phrase, Robert Putnam calls the former bridging social capital, and the latter bonding social capital.[16]

These networks can be further separated into two types: organizational and quotidian. I called the first *associational forms* of civic engagement, and the second, *everyday forms* of civic engagement. Business associations, professional organizations of doctors, lawyers, teachers and students, reading clubs, film clubs, sports clubs, festival organizations, trade unions, and political parties are some of the examples of associational forms. Everyday forms of engagement cover routine interactions of life such as whether Hindu and Muslim families visit each other, eat together, jointly participate in festivals, and allow their children to play together in the neighborhood. Both forms of engagement, if robust, promote peace: and their absence or weakness opens up space for communal violence. Of the two, the associational forms turn out to be more robust than everyday engagement, especially when confronted with attempts by politicians to polarize ethnic communities. Vigorous associational life, if intercommunal, acts as a serious constraint upon the polarizing strategies of political elites.

Why should this be so? Two links connect civic life and ethnic conflict. First, prior and sustained contact between members of different communities allows communication between them to moderate tensions and preempt violence when such tensions arise due to riots in a nearby city or state; distant violence or desecration reported in the press or shown on television; rumors planted by politicians or groups in the city to arouse communal bitterness and passions; or provocative acts of communal mischief by the police, thugs, or youth. All of these can be equated with *sparks* that do not necessarily turn into *fires*. In cities of thick interaction between different communities, peace committees at the time of tension emerge *from below* in various neighborhoods; the local administration does not have to impose such committees on the entire city *from above*. Because of mutual consent and voluntary involvement, the former is a better protector of peace than the latter. Such highly decentralized tension-managing organizations kill rumors, remove misunderstandings, and often police neighborhoods. If prior communication across communities does not exist, such organizations do not organically emerge from below. They are typically imposed from above, and the committees from above do not work well because their politician members, though inducted for purposes of peace, are normally already committed to polarization and violence for the sake of electoral benefit. Their presence on peace committees is often merely symbolic.

Second, in cities that have associational integration as well, not just everyday integration, the foundations of peace become stronger. In such settings, even those politicians who would, in theory, benefit from ethnic polarization find it hard to engender ethnic cleavages, arouse widespread bitterness, and instigate violence. Without a nexus between politicians and criminals, big riots and killings are highly improbable. If unions, business associations, middle class associations of doctors and lawyers, film clubs of poorer classes, and at least some political parties are integrated, even an otherwise mighty politician-criminal nexus is normally unable to break existing intercommunal links. Everyday engagement in the neighborhoods may not be able to stand up to the violence of gangs protected by powerful politicians, but unions, associations, and the integrated cadres of some political parties—those who unlike the polarizers are not interested in ethnic conflict—become bulwarks of peace in two ways: their local strength convinces those who would benefit from violence that engineering riots is beyond the realms of possibility, and even if violent cadres of polarizing parties and the thugs associated with them do try, they are prevented from instigating riots. Integrated organizations constitute a forbidding obstacle for even politically shielded gangs. When associational integration is available, the potential space of destructive and violent action simply shrinks.

Civic links across communities have remarkable local or regional variation. Depending on how different communities are distributed in local businesses, middle-class occupations, parties, and labor markets, they tend to differ from place to place. As a result, even when the same organization is able to create tensions and violence in one city or region, it is unable to do so in another city or region where civic engagement crosses communal lines. Local and regional variation in ethnic violence, its uneven geographical spread, can thus be a function of civic engagement, which tends to vary locally or regionally.

This argument is diagrammatically presented in figure 1. It builds upon the metaphor of "sparks" (small clashes, tensions, rumors) and "fires" (riots) to make the point about the role of civil society. Intercommunal ties between Hindus and Muslims, not intracommunal ties among the Hindus or among the Muslims, are a strong bulwark of communal peace.

If towns and cities were organized only along intra-Hindu or intra-Muslim lines, the odds of fires breaking out, given sparks, were very high. In Indian cities, bonding social capital was highly correlated with Hindu-Muslim violence, but bridging ties could put out sparks very effectively, not allowing them to disrupt the local equilibrium of peace. The local organs of the state—the police and administration—simply worked better at riot prevention in integrated cities.

Islamic or Hindu religiosity was not the principal reason for riots in Indian cities. *Rise of religiosity was in evidence in both peaceful and violent cities, not simply in the latter.* In facilitating or preventing riots, the type of

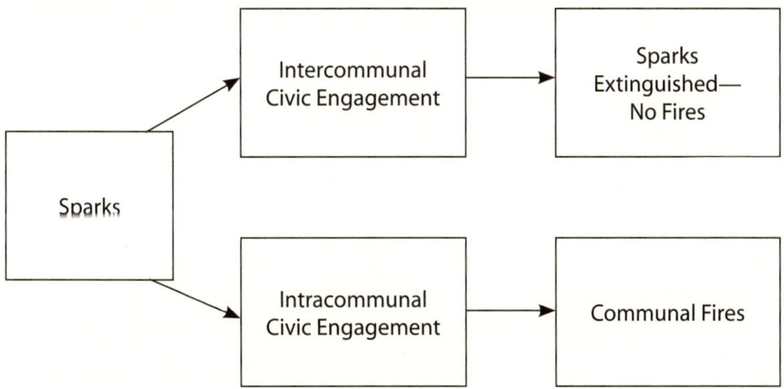

Figure 1. Civil Society and Ethnocommunal Violence

civic linkage—bridging or bonding, integrated or segregated—mattered most.

EXTENDING THE TERRAIN: DO ISLAM AND VIOLENCE GO TOGETHER?

The purpose of my new project is to (a) extend the comparative terrain and seek a multinational *and* multi-city comparison, and (b) to examine change over time, concentrating on cities that used to be violent but have become peaceful and *vice versa.* I have selected cities from Sri Lanka, Malaysia, and Indonesia.

In Sri Lanka, the Tamil-Sinhala riots are the object of study. I have chosen the cities of Colombo, Kandy, and Negombo. The first two had awful riots before 1983, Colombo more so than Kandy, but Negombo has always remained quiet. Moreover, none of the three cities has had riots since 1983, when a civil war began in the northern tip of the country. Since then, the armed forces of Sri Lanka and Tamil guerillas have killed one another in large numbers, but the Tamil and Sinhalese *civilians have not.* Interestingly, the customary sparks for riots—dead bodies of Sinhalese soldiers brought home to the south after ambushes up north; Tamil Tigers attacking the Temple of the Tooth in Kandy, a sacred Buddhist site—have been present in both periods, before and after 1983. But such provocations have been managed quite peacefully in all three cities after 1983, whereas they often led to violence before that.

In Malaysia, Kuala Lumpur, Penang, and Ipoh are the cities chosen. The first two experienced serious Malay-Chinese riots in the pre-1969 period, and the third had very little violence. All three have had no Malay-Chinese riots since 1969. Malaysia has had Malay-Chinese peace for over three decades now, something no observer of Malaysian politics in the 1960s predicted.

Indonesia suffered a lot of violence in the 1950s and 1960s, but not on the Muslim-Christian axis. The violence was primarily anti-Chinese. Since the mid-1990s, Muslim-Christian violence has spread to various parts of the country. The study concentrates primarily on changing Muslim-Christian relations over time and, secondarily, on anti-Chinese violence. Six cities are examined: Ambon, Poso, and Solo (all violence-prone, the third one less so than the first two); and Manado, Palu, and Yogyakarta (all peaceful).

In what ways is Islam involved in these conflicts, if at all? It should first be noted that, even though Sri Lanka is about 7 percent Muslim, the main axis of conflict does not involve Muslims. The ethno-religious profile of Sri Lanka can be presented in four parts: (a) 74 percent of Sri Lanka is *ethnically* Sinhalese, and 70 percent is *religiously* Buddhist; (b) 18 percent is ethnically Tamil and 15 percent religiously Hindu; (c) 7 percent is ethnically Moor and 7 percent religiously Muslim; and (d) 8 percent of the population is religiously Christian, consisting of several ethnicities. The primary clash is between (a) and (b). The Sinhalese, who are primarily Buddhist, and Tamils, who are primarily Hindu, have been locked in an internal political battle since the 1950s. The battle has periodically been violent and, since 1983, has taken the form of a civil war, which by most estimates has already killed over sixty thousand people.

Small Tamil-Muslim riots have taken place now and then, but Muslims in Sri Lanka have on the whole played a quiet role in politics. The Tamil Tigers, leading the civil war on the Tamil side, are Hindu by religious origin, not Muslim. Throughout the 1990s, suicide bombing became a hallmark of the politics of Tamil Tigers. Two heads of government, including one from India, and several major political figures have been killed by suicide bombers.

In Malaysia too, historically speaking, the principal cleavage has not involved Islam. The distribution of Malaysia's major ethnoreligious groups is as follows: (a) the ethnic Malays and other "indigenous" people constitute over 60 percent of the population, nearly all of whom are Muslim; (b) the ethnic Chinese are 24 percent of the population, subscribing to several religious faiths, mainly Confucianism, Buddhism, and Christianity; and (c) the ethnic Indians are 8 percent, mostly Hindu (but also containing a proportion of Muslims). Since independence, (a) and (b) have formed the principal cleavage, viewed and experienced almost entirely in ethnic, not religious, terms. The biggest riots in Malaysia—between the Malay and Chinese in 1969—had no religious content whatsoever. Malays as an ethnic group, not as a Muslim religious group, clashed with the Chinese, always defined ethnically or racially in Malaysia.

Islam has emerged in Malaysian politics in a big way over the last two decades. With isolated exceptions, it has principally been an issue *within* the Malay community.[17] It has taken the form of a political struggle between moderate Muslims, represented by the leading Malay political party, UMNO, and many of the more religious Muslims, represented by PAS. Establishment of an Islamic state in Malaysia has often been an avowed goal of PAS, whereas starting in the early 1980s, when Islam arose as a force in Malaysian politics, UMNO has sought to combine patronage of Islamic institutions with modern economic policies, especially in trade and infrastructure.[18] Since independence, UMNO has consistently ruled Malaysia at the federal center, though always in a coalition, whereas PAS has played an important role in only four out of thirteen states, all four at the northern end of the peninsula and all four having overwhelming Malay majorities (Kelantan, Terengganu, Kedah, and Perlis). PAS has not been able to penetrate states beyond these.

Though UMNO has of late started losing its legitimacy, it has historically been associated with Malaysia's remarkable rise from poverty in the 1960s to a middle-income country, one that has more or less banished poverty. It is still to be seen whether UMNO will lose power and a coalition of opposition parties, which might include PAS, will replace it before long.

What about Indonesia? Of late, Indonesia has been a focus of special attention in the international security and political circles. Islamic terrorist groups developed a foothold, Muslim-Christian relations became turbulent in some parts of the country, and the evidence that some Islamic groups had been involved in rioting as well as suicide bombing was unquestionable.[19] Indonesia is 88 percent Muslim, 8 percent Christian, 2 percent Hindu, and 1 percent Buddhist. Christians are not evenly spread, concentrated largely on the eastern islands like the Malukus and Sulawesi, which is also where the most gruesome Muslim-Christian rioting has taken place.

However, two important facts should be noted. First, as in India, collective violence is highly locally concentrated in Indonesia. As I have already reported, a mere fifteen districts (*kabupaten*), holding 6.5 percent of the country's total population, accounted for 85.4 percent of all deaths in collective violence between 1990 and 2003.[20] In most parts of the country, Muslims and Christians live peacefully together.

Second, while the Islamic terrorist networks of Indonesia have made international news, something much more important about Indonesian Islam remains buried in scholarly texts. NU (Nahdltul Ulama) and Muhhamadiya have historically been, and still are, the two biggest Islamic organizations of Indonesia. The former has anywhere between 25 and 30 million members, and the latter 20 to 25 million. These organizations run schools, universities, hospitals, libraries, and hostels. A very large number of Indonesian Muslims pass through these institutions, not through the violent networks.

What are the ideologies of these organizations? Neither subscribes to violent politics.[21] And neither endorsed the riots or the terrorist bombings. Indeed, NU, the biggest Muslim organization, does not want the state to be committed to Islam at all, saying Islam is a matter entirely for the personal realm. Abdurrahman Wahid, who was president of Indonesia between 1999 and 2001, also headed NU for a long time and has been its principal ideologue. He argues: "For me, an Islamic society in Indonesia is . . . treason against the constitution for it will make non-Muslims second class citizens."[22] In his view, propagated through the institutions of NU, Islam can flourish in Indonesia only in a nationalist and secular state that does not formally subscribe to Islam. A marriage of Islam and statecraft would militate against the authenticity and vigor of religious life.

Such organizations constitute the mainstream of Indonesian Islam. The violent networks are literally a fringe. The fringe might have acquired considerable firepower, but it has little popularity. It cannot match the hold that organizations like the NU and Muhammadiya have over Indonesian Muslims.

In short, in these countries, Islam, like the other religious systems of the world, is "multivocal," not "univocal."[23] To equate Islam with violence is untenable.

IS THE INDIAN HYPOTHESIS PORTABLE?

It should be noted first of all that some of the early findings already parallel those from India. Indonesian data have already been summarized above. Ethnocommunal violence tends to be highly *locally or regionally concentrated.* This was as true when Suharto's New Order violently ended in Indonesia in 1998 as it was in Malaysia in 1969, when the country experienced its worst riots since independence in 1957. In Sri Lanka, too, local concentrations were evident, whether in 1956 and 1958 or during 1977 to 1983, the worst phase of rioting on the island.

Does the Indian hypothesis—integrated civil society as a bulwark of peace—also work in other countries? Emerging materials suggest that we perhaps need an initial distinction in our theory between (a) multiethnic societies that have a history of segregated civic sites (unions, churches, schools, business associations, etc.)—for example, the United States, South Africa, Malaysia, and Sri Lanka—and (b) multiethnic societies where ethnic groups have led an intermixed civic life—for instance, India and Indonesia. Interethnic or intercommunal civic engagement may be a key vehicle of peace in the latter but, given the relative absence of common black-white civic sites in countries like the United States, there may not have been any space for interracial associational engagement historically, leading to puzzles about the precise mechanisms of peace in a different historical and social setting.

Indeed, if we think further about this distinction, it may actually be more accurate to say that some *groups* in a society may be historically segregated, not *societies* as a whole. In India, where political parties, unions, business associations, and voluntary agencies are by and large ethnocommunally quite mixed, segregation has historically marked relations between the "scheduled castes"—called *Dalits* in contemporary political discourse—and the "upper castes." Dalits were "untouchable" for centuries, and the upper castes ritually and socially "superior."[24] Historically, there have been no associational sites where the upper castes and the "untouchables" could come together, unlike the relationship between Hindus and Muslims, who had common civic spaces in many parts of India. Similarly, Protestants, Catholics, and Jews could eventually find common civic sites in the United States, but blacks and whites on the whole could not.[25]

"Self-policing," a mechanism of peace deductively proposed by Fearon and Laitin but yet to be empirically examined, may well be relevant to such segregated settings.[26] It means intraethnic, or intracommunal, policing of one's own youth, who are typically the earliest to strike, or strike back, at other groups. If exercised by elders, by an ethnic association, or by civic organizations such as churches, intraethnic policing may lead to the same result that intercommunal engagement does in India.

Both of these hypotheses—interethnic civic engagement and intraethnic self-policing—are civil-society based. The third and fourth hypotheses, also being explored in the new multicountry project, concern the state. One must remain open to state-level mechanisms, especially (a) if a state develops capacities to intervene quickly and effectively as ethnic *sparks* emerge, preventing their transformation into *fires*, or (b) the state introduces public policies and implements them, bringing a sense of justice or fulfillment to an aggrieved community, reducing thereby the odds of the very emergence of sparks. It is hard to imagine that, in political life, sparks can fully be prevented, but the idea is worth exploring nonetheless.

These remarks, of course, should not be construed to mean that in times of ethnic conflict, the state plays only the two roles identified above. States in different parts of the world are known to have played two other kinds of roles. Sometimes states inflame riots, siding clearly with one of the two ethnic groups in contention; and at other times, they simply tolerate riots, taking very little action even as the embers of violence burn ferociously.[27] Consider an example from India, though some other examples can also be given.[28]

In March and April of 2002, awful Hindu-Muslim violence took place in the Indian state of Gujarat.[29] From available accounts, it is clear that the state government not only made no attempt to stop the killings, but it also condoned them.[30] That the government "officially encouraged" anti-Muslim violence cannot be conclusively proved on the basis of the evidence provided by newspaper reports, though later research and inquiry commissions may well come to that definitive judgment. At this point, what is unquestionable is that the state actively condoned revenge killings instead of stopping them, which was constitutionally required.

The statements of nongovernmental organizations (NGOs) most closely associated with the Gujarat state government were highly indicative. According to the chief of the Vishva Hindu Parishad (VHP), Gujarat was "the first positive response of the Hindus to Muslim fundamentalism in 1,000 years."[31] Organizations like the VHP believe that the Bharatiya Janata Party (BJP) government did exactly what was required: namely, allowing violent Hindu retaliation against the Muslims, including those who had nothing to do with the mob that originally appeared to have torched two cars of a train, carrying Hindu pilgrims, in the Gujarati town of Godhra, an event that started the rioting. From a liberal perspective as well as, more importantly, constitutional perspectives, it is not the job of the government, whatever its ideological persuasion, to stoke public anger against it own citizens or to allow the public to express itself violently, regardless of the provocation. No elected government that has taken an oath to protect lives of its citizens can behave the way criminal gangs do, thirsting for a tit-for-tat. But that is what happened. More than a thousand people died.

The state can, thus, play three distinct roles: riot-inhibiting, riot-tolerating, and riot-inflaming. Needless to add, it is when the state plays the first role, usually constitutionally required, that it directly contributes to ethnic peace, not otherwise.

EMERGING DIRECTIONS

Though the new project is not yet completed, the city-level evidence from it has started coming in. Some materials clearly go in the direction of the Indian hypothesis; others do not. To illustrate this divergence, I will briefly summarize Sri Lankan materials first, and then concentrate at greater length on the emerging Malaysian results.

As I have already noted, of the three Sri Lankan cities, Colombo,

Kandy, and Negombo, the last has never had Tamil-Sinhala rioting. Negombo is a mere hour and a quarter away from the heart of Colombo city, where rioting during 1956, 1958, and 1977–83 was frequent. In 1983, riots in Colombo, with the involvement of the state, took the form of gruesome pogroms, touching off violence in many parts of the island. Even at that time, Negombo experienced some arson, but no riots.

Interviews make it clear that Negombo is exceptionally ethnically integrated. The most striking local institution is the Catholic Church. Like elsewhere in Sri Lanka, the Tamils and Sinhalese are ethnically distinct in Negombo, but unlike elsewhere, most Tamils and Sinhalese in that town share the Catholic faith. The Church brings the two ethnic groups together and has historically provided bridging social capital, which has developed enduring, organic roots. Moreover, there also exist a whole array of integrated organizations—business, labor, middle class—in the town. Negombo thus supports the Indian hypothesis about the role of civic integration in promoting ethnic peace. Unfortunately, it is one of very few towns where such integration between the two leading ethnic communities exists. Most Tamils and Sinhalese in Sri Lanka are Hindu and Buddhist respectively, not Christian. On the whole, religion does not play a bridging role in Sri Lanka, and other aspects of social life of the masses also do not.

The city-level results from Malaysia are also striking. While it is not yet unambiguously clear what explains Malay-Chinese peace since 1969, it is already obvious that the Indian hypothesis—civic integration as a foundation of ethnic peace—is not applicable. The Malay and the Chinese in Malaysia continue to be highly segregated, both in everyday life and in organizations.

To put the matter in perspective, let us compare the city of Kuala Lumpur (KL), the site of Malaysia's worst Malay-Chinese riots in 1969 but enjoying Malay-Chinese peace ever since,[32] with Calicut, one of the peaceful cities in the Indian study. In Calicut, the mass survey was conducted in 1995, and in KL, in 2005. The sampling methodologies were roughly similar.

Whereas nearly 83 percent of sampled Hindus and Muslims in Calicut reported "eating together *often*," in KL that proportion is 1.8 percent, and if added to "eating together *sometimes*," the total is only 8 percent. Nearly 90 percent of the Calicut sample had reported that Hindu and Muslim children played together in the neighborhood, the proportion in KL is 15 percent. About 84 percent of Calicut Hindus and Muslims visited each other socially; only 20 percent of the KL Malay and Chinese reported doing so.

In Calicut, a huge proportion of associations and civic organizations—for businessmen, labor, middle-class professionals—were integrated. In KL, only 3 percent of the sample said that the business organizations they had joined were mixed; only 2 percent reported being in mixed labor organizations; a mere 2.3 percent were in mixed middle-class professional organizations; and finally, only 1.8 percent, 5.7 percent, and 1.4 percent, respectively, said that the NGOs, party organizations, and neighborhood associations in which they had participated were mixed.

In short, both in quotidian and organizational life, KL is a highly segregated city. Two more points should be noted. KL is Malaysia's most cosmopolitan city. If anything, the prediction is that the eventual statistics will show an even lower level of integration in the two other Malaysian cities selected for the project.

Second, the current trends in group interaction are quite consistent with historical patterns. Early in the twentieth century, Furnivall had described Malay society as a place where different ethnic groups lived mostly separately, at best meeting in the marketplace for buying and selling. A careful study published in the 1970s had also concluded that "despite considerable changes in the city's ethnic composition, segregation of racial groups continues," the few upper-class neighborhoods of KL being the only exception.[33]

Despite remarkably little integration, Malay-Chinese peace in KL since 1969 has had its longest run for over a century. Most observers argue that it is the capacity of the state to nip tensions in the bud, or its policy performance, that accounts for the long peace. [34] Further research will show whether this explanation is correct.

Meanwhile, it should be noted that the government of Malaysia does not think state-level measures alone can continue to ensure peace, even if they have by now. Considering Malaysia's racial peace fragile, the government has launched a new drive aimed at societal integration. Rukun Tetangga, neighborhood-level committees, are the principal organizational vehicle for the drive. Expecting that they will bring the three races—the Malays, the Chinese, the Indians—together in everyday life, the government aims to cover the entire country with such committees over time. Presumably, once put in place by government, they will acquire a life of their own. According to a 2003 article in the *Straits Times*:

> National Unity Department director general Abdul Rashid Sahad said racial polarization in the workplace is becoming a worrying trend in the country. He said the tendency of workers to stick within their own community is gradually infiltrating workplaces, which is unhealthy for a multiracial country like Malaysia.
>
> In an effort to achieve "zero racial conflict" this year, the department has approved grants for Rukun Tetangga and public education programs, particularly those targeting the urban population, on the sensitivities of various races. Rukun Tetangga (RT) is a neighborhood watch group run by residents in housing estates to combat crimes and to promote racial integration. Abdul Rashid said the government hopes to set up 3,000 RTs to serve 7.5 million people by the end of the year, and eventually increase this to 4,800 for 12 million people by 2010.[35]

If such anxieties can emerge in a semi-democracy like Malaysia, which can deploy a lot of coercion in handling ethnocommunal relations, bridging social capital, especially of the organizational kind, should be considered even more important for ethnic peace in multiethnic democracies. Democracies do not easily get the option of regulating group relations by state *diktat*. In 1971, Malaysia could, by force, make affirmative action pro-Malay majority and could outlaw any discussion of it. Other ethnic groups simply had to accept the new rules favoring the Malays, whether they agreed or not. Such decisions often lead to serious, even violent, contention in democracies. Open discussion on policy can not normally be outlawed in democracies. Even Malaysia is beginning to feel the heat of late.

CAN THE STATE HELP THE EMERGENCE OF INTEGRATED CIVIL SOCIETIES?

It is often suggested that civil society, being a non-state sphere of collective life, depends entirely on citizen initiatives and is not something that the state either can build or should try to. Case evidence suggests that the story is more complicated and that the state can play a positive role. Consider an example.

Bhiwandi, a town just outside Bombay, India, was infamous for Hindu-Muslim riots in the 1970s and 1980s in which nearly two hundred lives were lost. The turning point was the arrival in June 1988 of a police chief for three years. In those three years, Bhiwandi was transformed from a town notorious for its capacity for rioting to one that could meticulously work for, and keep, communal peace, even in the worst of times, as it did between 1988 and 1993 and again in 2002. The key was building Hindu-Muslim contacts in an organized way and around common issues of concern. Peace has prevailed since 1988.

The town of Bhiwandi is a rather unlikely site for healthy and robust civic engagement. A center of small textile industry, most of which exists in the informal sector, Bhiwandi is full of "sprawling hutment colonies, narrow streets, the never-ceasing rattling of powerlooms," and "the town's civic amenities are bursting at the seams under the increasing demands of the shanties mushrooming all round."[36] Hindus and Muslims tend to live in segregated neighborhoods.

Undeterred by this setting and the town's history of violence, the police chief argued that instead of fighting the fires when they broke out, it was better for the police to bring Hindus and Muslims together to create mutual understanding. The aim was to set up durable structures of peace. If the Hindus and Muslims could meet each other often enough and discuss common problems, a reservoir of communication and perhaps trust would be created, which in turn would play a peacemaking role at the time of communal tensions. Thinking that "to be forewarned is to be forearmed,"[37] the police chief decided to put together neighborhood committees (*mohalla samitis*) for the whole town under his supervision.

Since segregated living was the norm in the town, each committee covered two neighborhoods and consisted of an equal number of Hindus and Muslims, selected on the basis of local knowledge. The committee members were those who "wielded considerable influence in their respective neighborhoods (*mohallas*) and had a clean record."[38] Special care was taken to ensure that "no communalist or known criminal," lacking a "genuine desire for peace," was selected. For every two or three committees, one police officer was appointed to act as liaison officer. Wherever available, the committee members included highly respected professionals, like doctors and lawyers. But in the poorest neighborhoods, where no such professionals were present, the committees consisted of "coolies and even housewives." Whether professionals, coolies, or housewives, the only condition for committee members was that they be respected by their neighbors for probity and goodwill, for which local knowledge was used, and have no criminal records, for which police data was consulted.

Seventy such committees were created to cover the entire town. They would discuss "matters of mutual concern."[39] They would meet as and when necessary, typically at least once a week but daily in times of tension, with a police officer presiding. And as time wore on, they turned out to be so successful that even nonmembers started attending important meetings, thus broadening "the base of mutual confidence."

During 1988–92, the nationwide mobilization, sponsored by the Hindu nationalists, for the destruction of the Baburi mosque was at its peak. As a consequence, communal tensions in much of India were high, and there were many moments of tension and bitterness in Bhiwandi as well. But "when passions ran high . . . , members on both sides came together and voluntarily undertook the task of patrolling the streets for nights on end. Rumors were suppressed on the spot and rumor-mongers handed over to the police . . . [As a result], the evil-doers preferred to lie low, . . . [and] were totally isolated by the constant vigilance against them by committee members."[40] Not a single life was lost.

In 2002, the neighboring state of Gujarat had brutal anti-Muslim riots. As the Gujarat riots raged, the head of a rather extreme Hindu nationalist organization, Bajrang Dal, was murdered in the town of Bhiwandi. The suspicion was that Muslims had attacked him to avenge the killings of Muslims by Hindu nationalist mobs in Gujarat. Again, tensions emerged, but only to subside. No riots broke out in Bhiwandi.

What should one conclude from this example? The Bhiwandi experiment, in particular, questions the idea, widely held in some circles, that there is an adversarial relationship between the state and civil society. Civil society is a *non*-state, not an *anti*-state, space of our life, whose vigor can be, though is not necessarily, promoted by the state. Civil society is typically anti-state when the state, by design or unintended consequence, begins to undermine civic life, not if it does not. Because civic linkages were forged on the initiative of the local organ of the state, the Bhiwandi experiment suggests fruitful possibilities of a state–civil society synergy for stemming endemic violence. With a strong civic edifice in place, the state can prevent riots with considerable ease. Organizationally integrated towns are simply easier to police in times of communal tensions, as helpful information travels quickly from civil society to local state organs and the two work synergistically. Sparks are put out before they become fires. Some other towns have of late followed the Bhiwandi model of neighborhood committees, reporting considerable success.[41]

Of course, the fact that the state in Bhiwandi facilitated and nurtured autonomous civil society organizations does not mean that states usually do so. Twentieth-century Latin American history is full of examples of corporatist organizations—business associations, workers unions, peasant organizations—created by the state primarily to serve the state's ends.[42] Corporatist structures do not allow autonomy from the state, the hallmark of a true civil society.

In short, while the state can indeed aid the evolution of civil society organizations, the Bhiwandi example should not be viewed as a normal course of state action in the developing world. Typically, organization creation of this kind requires a democratic polity. Authoritarian polities tend not to encourage autonomous civil society organizations, even if they want ethnic integration. Yugoslavia under Tito is known to have favored ethnic integration, but even as the softest Communist state, it did not allow organizations autonomous of the state.[43]

I have made two related arguments in this essay. First, ethnic integration in civic life, especially in organizations, is a most promising, if not the only, foundation of ethnic peace, a point not recognized in the literature until recently. Even when it is believed that the government can procure peace through administrative or policy measures, as in Malaysia, there are doubts, even in government quarters, that such peace may not last without civic integration. There are, of course, other ways to peace in multiethnic societies. The consociational experiments in Europe are diametrically opposed to my arguments about integrated civil societies. But as the vast literature on consociationalism shows, consociation experiments require certain preconditions for success; they are not generalizable.[44] My arguments here also should not be construed to imply that integrated civil societies are either always available or can be easily created. But once created and institutionalized, their implications for peace should be obvious.

Second, my argument about Islam is a specific version of the larger argument above. It is often argued, or assumed, that Islam as a religion has an integral relationship with communal violence. In the countries covered by my research, this argument does not hold. Whether Muslims are involved in large-scale violence is not a function of Islamic religiosity per se but of the kinds of links built between them and the other communities.

CHAPTER TWO

Debating Secession Peacefully and Democratically

The Case of Canada

RICHARD SIMEON

Studies of democratic breakdown or ethnic conflict tend naturally to focus on cases of failure and ask why. This chapter asks whether there may be lessons for others in the case of success. The case is Canada.

This is not to suggest that Canadian democracy represents some sort of ideal state. Canadians vigorously debate their "democratic deficit," focused on issues such as a first-past-the-post electoral system that seriously distorts the relationship between seats and votes and exaggerates regional differences, a Westminster-based parliamentary system that puts too much power in the hands of the prime minister, a system of intergovernmental relations that too often excludes the public, and so on. Canadians also worry about declining electoral turnout and citizen engagement, especially among younger citizens.[1] This chapter focuses on one thing that Canada does appear to have done especially well: the accommodation and management of difference.

Canadian democracy faces the task of managing three distinct dimensions of "deep diversity."[2] The first and most important, in the simple sense that only it has the potential of breaking the Canadian union, is language. Canada is a binational federation. French-speaking Canadians make up about a quarter of the population; they are heavily concentrated in Canada's second largest province, Quebec, where they constitute more than four-fifths of the population. Quebecers have a strong sense of national identity and a rich, distinct, and autonomous civil society. Managing the relationship between Quebec and the Rest of Canada, itself highly diverse, has been the fundamental challenge facing the Canadian polity since its inception in 1867.[3]

Second, Canada, like Australia, New Zealand, and many countries in Latin America, has an indigenous Aboriginal population, which has been historically exploited and marginalized. In recent years Aboriginal Canadians—the "First Nations"—have become politically mobilized in the search for self-government, land rights, and compensation for past injustice.

Third, Canada is a multicultural country. Canada has perhaps the highest rate of (legal) immigration in the world and one of the highest rates of foreign-born population. Today, most newcomers are of non-Western background (following a long history of racially discriminatory immigration policy), and immigrants tend to settle overwhelmingly in a few large urban centers. The Canadian response has been to emphasize the "mosaic" over the "melting pot." The Constitution and the Multiculturalism Act declare multiculturalism to be a fundamental defining characteristic of the country.[4]

In this chapter, however, I focus on the French-English, or Quebec-Canada, dimension of Canadian diversity.

"Success" in managing political divisions is, of course, a highly relative term. It is also contested. For most Canadians outside Quebec, success is defined by maintaining national unity and intergovernmental harmony. But almost half of Quebec citizens—and probably a majority of its francophone population—continue to support a sovereign Quebec and feel the Canadian federation to be a straitjacket that constrains the ability of the Quebec government to act as the primary government of a distinct nation. They would define success either as full recognition of Quebec's distinctiveness within the federation (the Quebec federalist position), or as the achievement of sovereignty (the position of the Indépendantiste Parti Québécois, or PQ).

By "success," in the context of this chapter, I do not mean victory for either side in this debate. Rather, I refer to the striking fact that a debate about the very future of the country as a single political entity has been conducted vigorously since the early 1960s in a democratic and peaceful manner.

CANADA AND QUEBEC

In 1995, Quebec voters came within a hair's breadth (less than one percent of the vote in a province-wide referendum) of choosing to opt for the status of a sovereign nation, which would be combined in an "economic and political partnership" with the remainder of Canada. While the sovereignty movement had existed since the 1960s, and the Parti Québécois had first formed a government in 1976, the close result led many to believe for the first time that secession might actually happen. And with that came the realization that the country was woefully unprepared to deal with the political and economic consequences of a breakup.

A series of earlier constitutional negotiations had failed to find agreement on a formula that could recognize Quebec's distinct status as the primary government of Quebecers. Canadians outside Quebec had come to believe strongly in the idea of "provincial equality," and many followed former prime minister Pierre Trudeau in arguing that recognition of special status would constitute the first step down a slippery slope that would inevitably lead to secession—if not sooner, then later.[5]

Following the close call in the 1995 referendum, the federal government became convinced that it was essential to clarify the rules of the game that should accompany the debate on secession. In particular, it believed that the question that had been put to Quebecers was unfairly stacked by offering the accompanying promise of continued "partnership." "Partnership" would require the consent of the Rest of Canada. Moreover, the federal government argued, no decision as profoundly important as this should be made by a simple majority of Quebecers, acting alone. English-speaking Quebecers and immigrant groups (allophones) remained deeply hostile to independence, and some spoke of a further partition of Quebec were sovereignty to be achieved. Quebec's Aboriginal community held its own referendum, with 95 percent voting for continued membership in the Canadian state.

Quebec leaders argued that the standard democratic rule is "fifty percent plus one." Once that was achieved, negotiations to complete the separation should begin. Federalists argued that fundamental constitutional change almost everywhere requires the consent of "super-majorities," and that the interests of minorities in Quebec—English speakers, Aboriginal peoples, and allophones—could not be ignored. Nor could the economic and political interests of Canadians in the rest of the country be left out of the equation.[6] Hence the federal government submitted a "reference" question to the Supreme Court of Canada, asking it to rule on the issue of whether any province had the right to secede unilaterally, either under existing Canadian constitutional law or under international law governing self-determination.

The court concluded that neither source of law provided a right of unilateral secession. It noted that the Canadian Constitution is silent on the matter, and that in international law, the right to self-determination depends on whether the claimant nation suffers from oppression by the majority. This was patently not the case in a democratic Canada in which, indeed, French-speaking Canadians have played a central role in national politics.

But the court went on to say that in the event that Quebec were to vote for secession "by a clear majority," and on a "clear question," then the Rest of Canada would have a "constitutional obligation" to negotiate the matter. The court found the justification for this in its analysis of the fundamental principles underpinning the Constitution—democracy, federalism, constitutionalism and the rule of law, and respect for minorities. These must guide any secession process, although how they were to be operationalized remained unclear.[7]

This was a fundamentally important decision for Canada. For the first time it was now acknowledged that secession is constitutionally possible but that it could only happen in an orderly and constitutionally valid process. Both sides saw some support for their position in the judgment, and both claimed victory.[8]

The federal government followed this decision with the Clarity Act,[9] designed to clarify the terms under which a referendum could trigger a negotiation process. It asserted that the federal Parliament would reserve to itself the judgment whether the referendum question was fair and whether the majority was sufficient to warrant negotiations. Quebec responded with its own legislation asserting the right of Quebec to secede on its own decision and with a simple majority. Whether and how two societies so deeply intertwined could negotiate their separation remains deeply uncertain.

In the first decade of the twenty-first century, the sovereignist movement appeared to be in a decline. A federalist Liberal government was in power at the provincial level; the sovereignist Bloc Québécois, which operates at the national level, seemed without direction. While many continued to support independence, the passion appeared to have waned. The stage seemed set for an exploration of more informal ways for Quebec to develop within the context of Canadian federalism, with perhaps greater flexibility on both sides. But by 2004, the Liberal government in Quebec was highly unpopular, and the Bloc Québécois staged a strong comeback in the federal election. By 2008, the long-governing Liberal Party had been replaced by a minority Conservative Party government. Seeking to strengthen its support in Quebec in pursuit of a majority government, it responded to Quebec concerns by espousing a decentralist "open federalism" that included major fiscal transfers to the provinces and a parliamentary resolution that for the first time affirmed that Quebec constituted a "nation" within Canada.[10]

DEBATING SECESSION

Canada has thus experienced a powerful secessionist movement for four decades. At several points, the survival of the country as a unified federation has been in doubt. The debate has often been highly contentious and divisive. But what is most striking from a comparative perspective is the cardinal fact that the debate has been conducted with remarkable civility. The only time at which the debate turned violent was a brief episode in 1970 (the "October Crisis"), when a small group of radical Quebec separatists kidnapped a British diplomat and then kidnapped and killed a federalist Quebec cabinet minister. The federal and Quebec governments responded with a dramatic invocation of the War Measures Act. The episode was quickly over. The Front du Libération du Quebec soon disappeared, and democratic advocacy of secession continued. Otherwise, the debate has been entirely democratic, nonviolent, and peaceful on both sides.

Given the frequency with which such movements in other countries descend into violence and civil war, it is worth asking what it is about the Canadian case that has permitted such a democratic debate on such a vital issue. No single variable or factor can account for this complex phenomenon. But a tentative answer would include the following considerations. I distinguish *cultural, historical, institutional,* and *contextual* factors.

CULTURES AND VALUES

Democratic Cultures

Both in Quebec and in the Rest of Canada, there is a powerful commitment to democratic values and to free and open discussion. This has meant that virtually no voices in the Rest of Canada have declared the secessionists to be "traitors" or "treasonous." None have argued that they should be denied the opportunity to express their ideas, elect a provincial government, and send separatist members of Parliament to Ottawa.[11] The result is that the separatist movement was never driven underground, never forced to the margins, never excluded. There was no need for it to resort to violent means. Credit for this must go to the tolerance of citizens and their leaders, both in Quebec and the Rest of Canada. It is also notable that few, if any, politicians outside Quebec have suggested that the secession of Quebec should be denied absolutely; all have accepted either tacitly or explicitly that their commitment to democracy might at some point mean that they would have to accede to secession. None has argued that the federation should, or could, be held together by coercion.[12]

This view has now been made part of Canada's constitutional law through the decision of the Supreme Court of Canada: in the Secession Reference (1998) it concluded that Canada is divisible under some conditions. The lesson is that the more open the democratic space, the greater the chances of a peaceful process, whatever the outcome.

Predominantly "Civic" Nationalisms

Given its historic attachments to Britain, its multiculturalism, and its regional differences, some wonder if there is such a thing as "English-Canadian" identity. In fact, there is a strong sense of national identity. But Canada's history as an immigrant society since its inception means that English-Canadian nationalism has never been rooted in an ethnic definition of the country. Nor has its conception of the country ever focused on a European-style conception of a Napoleonic unitary state. Thus while Canadians outside Quebec are deeply concerned to protect the Canadian political union, advocates of alternative arrangements, even fundamental ones, have not been considered fundamentally illegitimate.

The Quebec case is a bit more complex. First, Quebec nationalists strongly identify with Quebec as the primary object of loyalty. But not all such nationalists are "indépendantiste." In fact, opinions on the national question in Quebec range along a continuum—from those calling for a "renewed federalism" that would be more asymmetrical[13] and more decentralized, to those advocating sovereignty with a continuing association with the Rest of Canada, to those who want a fundamental break. Surveys continue to demonstrate that even those seeking independence retain strong attachments to Canada; that the preponderance of Quebec opinion is found in the middle categories (sovereignty-partnership and renewed federalism); and that status quo federalists and out-and-out separatists are on the margins.[14]

As a result, attitudes expressed in public opinion surveys vary widely depending on the wording of the question. As in the former Czechoslovakia, where many voters seemed quickly to reconsider their position, a "yes" result in a sovereignty referendum might be equally ambiguous, perhaps triggering deep misunderstandings on both sides.

The Québécois identity is indeed rooted in language, seeing Quebec as a predominantly French-speaking society. Support for sovereignty is overwhelmingly concentrated in the francophone majority in the province. Nevertheless, Quebec is also a diverse and increasingly multicultural society, and both in its policies and its rhetoric the PQ vehemently asserts that its nationalism is also an inclusive rather than an exclusive one.[15]

I do not wish to exaggerate this point: there is hostility to bilingualism among some elements in English-Canadian society, and some Quebec nationalists espouse a more ethnic model of Quebec identity. Nevertheless it is striking that such views are considered illegitimate on both sides of the linguistic divide. When an embittered PQ premier Jacques Parizeau blamed the narrow defeat of 1995 on "money and the ethnic vote," he was condemned on both sides of the linguistic divide and immediately lost his position. Thus, despite deep differences on the desirable political structure, the debate is not cast in terms of mutually hostile ethnic identities.

Common Political and Social Values

The fundamental difference between Quebec and the Rest of Canada lies in language—in the predominance of French in Quebec and of English elsewhere. There are some other cultural differences—such as a slightly more social democratic approach to the role of the state in Quebec and perhaps a stronger emphasis on a more European "associative" or consensual model of policymaking. But these appear to be relatively minor differences—certainly no larger than the differences that exist among the other provinces. Indeed, what is more striking is the *similarity* between Quebecers' views about the role of the state and public policy and those of other Canadians. Thus the Canada-Quebec debate is not one of competing and antithetical worldviews. These are two very similar societies in social and economic terms, seeking to manage their political relationship.

HISTORICAL LEGACIES

Canada has always been a "negotiated country." In the first encounters between Europeans and indigenous peoples, the development of the fur trade required an accommodation between the two groups. When Britain defeated France and took control of what is now Canada, Britain agreed that the French-Canadians could retain their Roman Catholic religion, their language, and their distinct pattern of civil law.[16] Confederation in 1867 was also negotiated among the British North American colonies; it included the peaceful separation of the united colony of "Canada" into two new provinces—Ontario and Quebec. Similarly, Canada's independence from Britain came about not through revolution but through an incremental step-by-step process that is, in minor respects, still not complete.[17] Thus, in important ways, the Canadian tradition is one of negotiation and accommodation rather than confrontation and contestation. This tradition has powerfully shaped the nature of the secession debate. Moreover, traditions of accommodation that have developed with respect to older divisions can provide a template—if not specific solutions—for responses to newly salient differences.

For example, the logic of federalism—with shared sovereignty and multiple identities—can provide a broad framework for the accommodation of Aboriginal self-government within Canada.

INSTITUTIONAL FACTORS
A Multi-unit Federation

The dynamics of secession might play out very differently were Canada to be a two-unit federation where Quebec faced a cohesive English Canada. In fact, Quebec plays a dual role in the federation: it is simultaneously one of "two nations" and one of ten provinces (and three territories).[18] This has meant that only on a few occasions has Quebec been fully isolated. These moments—such as Quebec's rejection of a 1982 constitutional settlement that did not address Quebec's aspirations—have indeed been the most crisis-ridden periods in Canadian politics. But on most contentious issues, Quebec has had allies among the other provinces—with Ontario, its large neighbor, on fiscal and economic issues; with the western provinces on issues to do with resisting federal "intrusions" into provincial jurisdiction; and with the Atlantic provinces with which it shares an interest in the continuation of regional economic equalization programs. Quebec's consistent assertion of provincial autonomy has also helped promote strong provincialist strategies in other provinces, especially in wealthy provinces such as Alberta. The causal arrow runs both ways: a decentralized Canada helps accommodate Quebec; the presence of Quebec ensures that Canada's federalism will be highly decentralized. In 2003, at the suggestion of a Quebec federalist government, the provinces and territories created a new Council of the Federation, bringing together their first ministers. It has been highly successful in bridging interprovincial differences in population, wealth, and region, and in forging a provincial alliance in negotiations with Ottawa. A federal-provincial accord (on health care, 2004) explicitly recognizes "asymmetrical federalism." All of this further integrates Quebec into the Canada-wide fabric of politics and reduces the sole focus on the Ottawa-Quebec confrontation. The lesson is that polarization is less likely to occur when the federation has multiple units.[19]

Provincial Autonomy: Building Out

The Canadian federal system has provided a high degree of autonomy to Quebec (and other provinces). Indeed one federal minister has described the government of Quebec as the most powerful subnational government in the world. The danger here, of course, is that with such a powerful provincial government, it may seem only a small further step to full secession. But the positive side is that the federation has been flexible enough to accommodate a great deal of the nation-building impulse (*maitres chez nous*) of successive Quebec governments—whether in measures to preserve and promote the French language in the province, to pursue economic development, or to establish a distinctive social policy. Quebec political leaders have often described federalism as a straitjacket blocking Quebec's national aspirations and have seen the federal government as bent on centralization. In fact, Quebec governments have a wide range of jurisdictional and fiscal resources at their disposal. And successive federal governments have frequently tempered any desire to exert greater central control over important policy areas with the realization that such action would alienate Quebec. Thus, while Quebec has been unable to achieve constitutional recognition of its distinct status, it has had a wide scope for initiative and discretion within Canada. And despite the inability to agree on asymmetrical federalism in the Constitution, a high degree of informal asymmetry prevails. The lesson is that decentralization, to give minority groups control over matters important to their identity and survival and to protect them from the imposition of the will of the majority, can provide an effective means of accommodation. Were it not constituted as a federation, Canada would almost certainly not exist as a country.

Integration at the Center: Building In

So far we have focused on the capacity of federalism to embrace autonomy as a major reason for the relative civility of the debate. Now we turn to the other side of the coin. Quebec and Quebecers have also been built into national political structures. This happens in many ways. At the most basic political level, it is virtually impossible to form a federal government in Canada without substantial support from Quebec. All governing parties in Canada are coalitions of varying interests, but Quebec is virtually always part of the winning coalition. With only brief interludes, all Canadian prime ministers since the 1960s have been Quebecers. In addition, a federal royal commission that reported in the 1960s found that francophone Quebecers were underrepresented in the most senior cabinet positions and in the senior public service and that virtually all those who were in the system were required to work in English. This underrepresentation has now been virtually eliminated. Canada is an officially bilingual country, and the federal Official Languages Act is designed to provide protection and services to linguistic minorities both in Quebec and in the Rest of Canada and to ensure strong francophone representation in the public service. Thus the "building out" of a high level of autonomy is accompanied by a large measure of "building in"—ensuring that Quebecers are linked to and participate in the countrywide government. This is why the secessionist movement has realized that it must couple its proposal for sovereignty with the notion of "partnership" or "association" if it is to have any chance of success in a referendum. The lesson is that autonomy for minority groups is one element in a larger accommodation, but equally important is the integration of the minorities into the central political system.[20]

The literature on the accommodation and management of diversity tends to fall into two camps. One camp argues that stability is to be found through the recognition, institutionalization, and empowerment of difference by means of federalism or other forms of consociationalism. The other argues that stability is to be found in institutions that create incentives for leaders to blur, crosscut, and transcend differences.[21] Both the successes and the failures of the Canadian model suggest that the right approach is and/and rather than either/or.[22]

The Role of an Independent Court

When the stakes of political conflict are high, an independent institution, trusted by all sides, can be of critical importance. The Supreme Court of Canada has played this role on several occasions.[23] After failed constitutional discussions in 1980, the federal government attempted to amend the Constitution unilaterally. A coalition of provinces brought the issue to the court. It found that while the precise letter of the law gave the federal government the requisite authority, a constitutional "convention" had arisen that required substantial provincial consent before an amendment could proceed. This decision forced the parties back to the bargaining table.[24] In 1998, following the closely decided referendum, the court again acted as mediator. The court has played a similarly critical role in laying the groundwork for negotiations between Aboriginal peoples and Canadian governments. The lesson is that accommodation is facilitated when there exist institutions that are above the fray, not captured by any side, and committed to critical constitutional values.

Caution about Constitutional Reform

Successive rounds of attempts to redefine Canada-Quebec relations in the Constitution (the last in 1992) have failed. Lack of consensus about some fundamental features of the country made these debates necessary; the same lack of consensus guaranteed their failure. It has, on the other hand, been much easier to find agreement—allowing for much de facto asymmetry—on specific policy issues. Following years of fruitless constitutional negotiation, including the two referenda in Quebec and a national referendum, on a complex package deal in 1992 (the Charlottetown Accord) both Canadians and Quebecers have tacitly agreed that constitutional bargaining and referenda are to be avoided unless absolutely necessary.[25]

CONTEXTUAL FACTORS

Distinct but Interdependent Societies

In many respects, language is fundamental. It sustains Quebec's distinctiveness and identity in many ways. For example, popular culture, the media, and associational life do take on the character of "two solitudes," with relatively few connections between Quebec and "English-Canadian" cultures and civil societies. But in other respects, Quebec and the Rest of Canada are deeply intertwined. Despite globalization and North American integration, economic linkages within Canada remain strong. Economic disparities between French-speaking Quebecers and English speakers, once considerable, have now been eliminated. While Quebec and English-Canadian civil societies are largely distinct, shared interests in fields from agriculture to rights for gays and lesbians create the conditions for considerable "bridging" social capital.[26]

Quebec, with provinces to its east and west, is not an easily severed outlier. This too moderates the intensity of the debate. Neither side wishes to threaten economic or other relationships that are critical to the well-being of both. This is why sovereignist proposals have always been accompanied by commitments to association or partnership. The lesson is that policymakers should emphasize building interdependencies among competing groups, stressing that the fate of each is bound up with the fate of the other. This perspective also suggests that it may be misleading to overemphasize the importance of common identities in maintaining unity. Common substantive or material interests may provide an important glue as well.

The Presence of the United States

In general, United States policy has assiduously avoided intervention in the Canadian debate. Nevertheless, both sides recognize that the United States has a major stake in political and economic stability of the country on its northern border, with which it is joined in the North American Free Trade Agreement. This too appears to have a moderating effect both on Quebec separatist strategies (one reason for the emphasis on continued association once independence is achieved) and on reactions in the Rest of Canada. The lesson is that unbiased external actors and a benign geographic neighborhood can mitigate domestic conflicts; biased outsiders are likely to exacerbate them.

Saying No to Violence

Finally, I return to the one case in which there was violence surrounding Quebec nationalism, in 1970. The reaction of the federal and provincial governments to the kidnappings and murder was swift and draconian. Emergency powers were invoked, troops deployed, many innocent persons arrested, and so on. Some, including this writer, felt at the time that the reaction was much too harsh. But perhaps the key fact in retrospect is that this assertion of authority was quickly followed by a return to normal, open, democratic politics. There was no continuing crackdown. The democratic space was quickly reopened. It thus became clear that violence would not be tolerated but that free expression, even of radical separatist views, would be fully accepted. Hence the violent movement quickly disappeared, and Quebec nationalism continued on the democratic path. The lesson is that while violence must be stopped, the channels for democratic politics must be kept open at the same time.

These and perhaps other factors appear to explain why Canada has been able to conduct a debate about secession—indeed about the very political future of a political entity called Canada—with remarkable civility and within the framework of peaceful, democratic politics. No single country can serve as a model for others, since the circumstances of each will differ. Canada has the particular advantage of addressing fundamental disagreements within the framework of an affluent economy and a fully consolidated democratic politics. Nor are there any guarantees that Canada will continue to manage its conflicts so successfully. An inexorable decline in the francophone proportion of the total population may well induce new strains; a populist challenge to the traditional Canadian politics of "elite accommodation" may also threaten settled arrangements.

More fundamentally, we cannot know what the reactions of Canadians would be in the days and months following a successful vote for secession in Quebec. This analysis suggests that the probable outcome would be a "velvet divorce" and that the two successor countries would each remain fully consolidated democracies. But it is risky simply to assume that calm reason would prevail; passion and circumstance might easily escalate tensions rapidly. For example, some English-speaking Quebecers have argued for "partition," saying that if Quebec can leave Canada, than they should be able to leave Quebec. This raises the specter of "ethnic cleansing." Aboriginal Canadians held their own referendum in Quebec in 1995, voting overwhelmingly to stay in Canada, seeing their concerns as the primary constitutional responsibility of the federal government. A flight of capital and a collapsed dollar could sow economic panic. However desirable a postsecession "partnership" might be in economic terms, there would likely be strong opposition in the Rest of Canada. And the future unity of the Rest of Canada, itself regionally divided, could not be guaranteed in the long term. Negotiating a peaceful secession would call for even greater tolerance and skill than negotiating accommodation. Thus Canadians should not complacently assume that they have the magic cure for managing conflict in divided societies.

Yet the Canadian pattern does suggest some conclusions that may be applicable elsewhere and, indeed, that seem to confirm some of the generalizations in the literature on management of conflict in divided societies.

First is the commitment to democratic values and tolerance. Mutual agreement on the democratic rules of the game is critical. Some minimal level of trust and respect is essential to civil debate. Equally important is to maintain, as much as possible, open, democratic spaces in which debate can occur rather than driving it to the political margins. The need to ensure that debates about political futures are carried out within the parameters of democracy, constitutionalism and the rule of law, and respect for minorities—the values espoused by the Supreme Court of Canada—is fundamental.

Moreover, the Canadian story suggests that several other factors help to achieve accommodation and to moderate conflict even when there is a strong commitment to greater autonomy for the minority. On the one hand, there needs to be a commitment to "building out," to ensuring that distinct minorities have a measure of self-government and empowerment to manage their own affairs. But on the other hand, it is vital to ensure minorities representation and voice at the center—a commitment to "building in"—to ensure that these minorities are included rather than excluded in the larger political system. A commitment to economic and political equality—"sharing"—across minority and majority groups so that cleavages do not continually overlap and reinforce each other is also highly desirable. The Canadian case also demonstrates the need to make sure that there will be some independent, nonpartisan bodies that will ensure commitment to democratic principles and the rule of law.

Also important to ensuring moderation is the mutual realization that whatever the outcome of the secession debate, closely linked societies will have to continue to coexist as neighbors and traders. They thus must not burn all their bridges.

What lessons can be drawn from Canada's long experience with debating secession? Canadians have not invented any magic formula that can easily be transferred. Indeed many aspects of the story told here are highly dependent on Canada's history and particular context. Canada's historical legacy as a negotiated country cannot be replicated; nor can democratic, civil, and tolerant political cultures be created overnight. Most countries facing similar secessionist tendencies exist in much more dangerous geographic neighborhoods. Few have Canada's economic security. The stakes of secession are indeed high in Canada, but they may be less than is the case in other countries. Yet the Canadian case also demonstrates some lessons that can be useful: the importance of general agreement on the rules of the game; the importance of independent third parties to mediate the conflict; above all the importance of developing institutions that combine autonomy for sub-state nations with their full representation at the center. All these can facilitate democratic debate, whatever its outcome.

PART TWO

Toward Creating and Controlling Democratically Usable Security Services

CHAPTER THREE

The New "Double Challenge"

Democratic Control and Efficacy of Military, Police, and Intelligence

FELIPE AGÜERO

Military or security forces today are more likely to endanger democracy by lessening its quality and depth than by threatening its outright and swift overthrow.[1] While the stability of new democracies is certainly not assured, the strongest concern lies with their ability to advance the rule of law and guarantee the basic liberties and needs of their citizens.[2] In regard to the armed forces, the police, and intelligence agencies, new democracies are often poorly prepared to face up to a double challenge: developing firm institutions for the democratic control of those services and turning them into effective tools for the protection and security of their citizens. The source of these difficulties is to be found not only in those services but also, and often primarily, in the inaction, complicit stance, or active encouragement of nondemocratic behavior by civilian actors in government or political society.[3]

Security agencies and military and police institutions inherited from authoritarian regimes were particularly adept at survival and reaccommodation, especially in those new democracies that resulted from negotiated transitions. Security forces in these cases retained high levels of autonomy and prerogatives,[4] as well as practices that contradicted democratic norms. Developing institutions that may help rein in these tendencies and assert control is one of the primary tasks of these new democracies, a task that demands leadership in delineating separate and well-defined missions for the different armed services at the same time that they are properly coordinated in the pursuit of a common purpose defined by the political leadership.

In cases where democratization followed not a negotiated transition but the settlement of armed conflict, officials had to wrestle with a different and more complex challenge, that of recreating institutions while simultaneously trying to provide for citizen security. The difficulties in facing this challenge often led to high levels of insecurity or to the deployment of poorly trained forces.[5]

The transitions literature highlighted the wisdom of sequencing tasks so that fragile and newly established democratic governments were not overwhelmed by simultaneously taking on many "urgent" challenges.[6] But many cases of democratic construction could not afford this luxury, better meant for cases where negotiation had allowed for large degrees of institutional continuity. In addition, for most new democracies, the persistence of problems of control in the face of security challenges demand simultaneity in the tasks of asserting control and pursuing reforms and modernization.

Threats are enhanced and multiplied by a context of strengthened transnational organized crime and international terrorism.[7] This aids the expansion of a perverse scenario with multifaceted impact, for instance, leading to inciting corruption of security forces and agencies; confusion of the lines separating military and police functions; and substantial increase in the public perception of insecurity, leading in turn to forceful but often short-sighted response. The result often found is a disregard for civil liberties in security forces and a distorting prioritization of security—a securitization of development, political, and social issues.

Problems facing the armed forces, the police, and intelligence agencies are tightly interconnected. A weak or ineffective police force will put pressure on officials to use the military in policing roles for which it is ill prepared or to militarize the police. The existence of several poorly controlled intelligence agencies may harm the professionalism of the military and police, and so on. Problems in this sector are in turn embedded in the larger context of developmental challenges and institutional features of society and politics. However, this interconnectedness seldom is appropriately considered by policymakers, and only recently has it begun to be subjected to scholarly analysis. Neither democratic political leaders nor social scientists concerned with democracy crafting have yet developed an integrated approach to capture this interconnectedness. The social sciences have maintained separate approaches to studying civil-military relations and defense, police, and judicial reform; the study of intelligence, especially, in lesser developed contexts, has been vastly overlooked. Nonetheless, out of practical need and recent reflection, these problems have begun to be addressed with concepts such as security sector reform that cut across narrow boundaries and allow for a comprehensive approach.[8] At the same time, the goals and the process of security sector reform have been more clearly connected to notions of human security and citizen security than to previous emphases on national security,[9] although as with all charged concepts, the concept of security sector reform has developed as a contested field subject to different definitions with quite different implications in terms of primary actors and policy substance and goals. First advanced by developed countries facing aid and assistance strategy dilemmas in conflict-laden areas in the South, these concepts are now utilized by actors everywhere.

However, threats to democracy that originate in state security actors and institutions are not limited to new democracies. In the case of older democracies, the corporate interests of the armed services, police, or intelligence agencies often translate into undue influence over policy, areas of autonomy that expand beyond acceptable limits, and resistance to outside control. Although older democracies count on stronger and more complex institutions, they vary in terms of their ability to succeed against those threats, displaying unequal zeal and institutional ability for democratic control. In addition, old democracies too suffer from serious gaps in attitudes and beliefs between individuals in society and members of the military and security services.

THE ARMED FORCES

The military, especially in new democracies, is one of the actors most prone to seeking high levels of autonomy, eluding submission to the authority of elected officials. Autonomy usually was retained from military-authoritarian regimes, but it was often expanded during or after democratic transitions. This occurred especially in cases in which the military was reassured after bureaucratic military rule, with new civilian authorities too weak to assert leadership and control and either too keen or left with little choice but to appease a restive military.

Latin America provides many illustrations.[10] In Brazil, for instance, the military saw its autonomy enhanced during the first phases of democratization. As it witnessed authoritarian rule gradually weaken and grow dysfunctional, the military reasserted itself during civilian rule to ensure high levels of autonomy, influence the political process, and retain prerogatives, many of which it would ultimately lose in the long run, but not without leaving a complex set of buffers to protect its autonomy in many domains.[11] In Chile, constitutional legacies from authoritarianism granted the military large levels of autonomy for fifteen years after the end of military rule. Military prerogatives included appointment of senators and participation in appointments to the constitutional court as well as denying the president the power to remove top chiefs. The set of constitutional guarantees for the military were not removed until the reforms passed in 2005 toward the end of the administration of President Lagos.[12] Even in Spain, among the starters of the Third Wave of democratization in southern Europe, a case that would rise to model status for its successful and peaceful transition to democracy, the military gained some autonomy and powers of contestation in the early phases of transition before it was reined in with audacious military and defense reforms.[13] Similar traits were found in Asia, as exemplified by cases as diverse as Pakistan and Thailand.[14]

Mexico, on the other hand, illustrates the risks for enhanced threat in the security sector that are made possible by the spaces and opportunities opened by political transition. The demise of civilian one-party rule, in which the military had been historically subdued, created new opportunities for reassertion of the military in a context of competing political leaderships and high demand for security as a result of highly organized and violent transnational criminal activity throughout its territory.[15]

In other cases of democratization, such as those following the demise of neopatrimonial rule, as in many African countries, military factionalism along ethnic lines or other sources of allegiance became both an opportunity and a major risk. In some places (Niger, Burundi) militaries blocked democratization in the 1990s, while in other places (Nigeria, Ghana), they were led to acquiesce.[16] However, the end of military rule, as in Nigeria, opened the way to increasing levels of societal violence, complicating attempts to reform the security sector.[17]

EXPRESSIONS OF AUTONOMY

Military autonomy is reflected in the most important areas of budgets, education, and justice. In regards to the definition of *budgetary* priorities and allocations, the military often eludes the scrutiny of congress and even of civilians in the executive power. As regards funding sources, some cases, as in Chile and more recently in Peru, assign the armed forces substantial resources directly and automatically as a fixed percent of revenue from commodity exports. In other cases, as in the Philippines, Indonesia, Thailand, and Ecuador, military-run businesses have proliferated, completely outside civilian control.[18] In the area of *education*, the military tends to elude supervision of national educational authorities or even top defense officials. The military has acquired in many countries complete autonomy to determine educational orientation and contents, as well as the ability to provide academic degrees, including for civilians in military academies or military-related universities. Resistance to what is perceived as outside interference in internal matters is based on the notion that the military is a unique and fully differentiated profession demanding emphasis on separate values that can only be nurtured and developed from within the services themselves. The military also considers itself the authority best entitled and equipped to define patriotism, honor, and other such concepts and to exert guardianship of the national interest.[19] Inclusion of human rights teaching in the curriculum became part of the military's insertion in new democratic regimes in those cases where gross violation of human rights had taken place under military rule, but these matters are often not supervised from outside or made consistent with prevailing views in society.

Just as with education, military *justice* remains a separate sphere in many cases, outside the jurisdiction of national courts, and military courts continue to have tuition over civilians. In cases of gross violations of human rights under previous military regimes, varying degrees of impunity have been observed, and violations under new democratic regimes, especially in routine public-order work, are far from fully eliminated. In many cases the military continues to assert tutelage over the police. Finally, it is telling that *state reform*, a concept and set of programs in place since the emergence of new democracies in the latest wave, sometimes meaning the accommodation of the public sector to market reforms or its adaptation to demands for accountability and participation, is seldom expanded to embrace reforms that would include a branch so critical to the state as the military, so as to adapt them to a more general reform trend aimed at greater efficiency and accountability. Here, as in other areas, main responsibility lies with political leadership more than with the military.

Older democracies face their own set of problems in the areas of control and accountability. Robin Luckham, for instance, has stated that "there is arguably greater democratic accountability within the security sector in new democracies like South Africa than obtains in many established democracies like India, France, or the United Kingdom."[20] In cases of large defense establishments, control is made harder by sheer bureaucratic size, where opportunities for shirking increase.[21] The relationship of the armed forces to the political system also makes it possible to skirt civilian directives by playing parts of the bureaucracy, or of government, against each other, hence increasing their autonomy, as has been the case in the United States.[22] Numerous studies also have warned about a growing gap between military and civilians regarding attitudes and beliefs.[23] In new democracies this gap is compounded by a continuous divide over views on human rights and their systematic violations by security forces under previous regimes. In view of the importance of these breaches, analysts have called for renewed attention to the importance of social, cultural, and educational aspects in military and society relations across all democracies, old and new.[24]

COUNTERING AUTONOMY

Autonomy from democratic control has been countered in a number of successful cases of military and defense reform. In some of them, reform followed the end of armed conflict, with international supervision, as in El Salvador, or through negotiated transition, as in South Africa, a case generally praised for the effectiveness and depth of its reforms. Nowhere, however, has reform been as thorough and successful as in Spain at the start of Third Wave democratization. The military there was removed from positions in government, saw its constitutional role redefined, and was subjected to complete control by a potent ministry of defense. The structure of the forces was reorganized, and military education and career paths rearranged according with goals of modernization and democratization.[25] Starting with the creation of an institutional edifice for leadership and control—centered in the creation or empowerment of a vigorous ministry of defense—reforms expanded to all other relevant areas so that autonomy was checked in favor of full submission to democratic authorities. All cases of success benefited from a favorable international climate and the help of international organizations, vast popular and political support, and an explicit determination by the leading political elites to pursue in-depth reforms. Other countries have embarked on similar attempts but have been unable to stay the course, with no civil society mobilization for reform and/or elites lacking the will or the ability to persist.[26] In addition to the absence of adequate institutions for leadership, control, and oversight, many countries have also had difficulty developing a cadre of civilian experts in security affairs, as well as independent research centers or think tanks to support their work.

The responsibility of democratic leaders in this area cannot be emphasized enough. The few fully successful cases have responded to a leadership willing to put effort and resources in reconceptualizing military, police, and intelligence policies in the new democratic milieus and sustaining these policies over time. On the contrary, cases of failure or only lukewarm and partial success often owe their shortcomings to leadership failures in conceiving and persistently pursuing the right kind of reforms more than to any other kind of "objective" constraint.[27]

INTERNATIONAL MILITARY RELATIONS

The international military relations of democracies become part of the problem if they result in reinforcing military autonomy. Weakness in civilian leadership has for many years allowed independent development of international relations of national militaries, as was reflected in the periodic armies' international conferences, for instance, in Latin America. Only recently, as a healthy attempt at civilian assertion, has that receded to the priority given to the conferences of defense ministers. But international climate is not always conducive to that assertion in the Inter-American region, given the consequences, perhaps unintended, of the role of the United States Southern Command in managing foreign and security policies toward the region. Civilian-led international networks that have been so crucial in other contexts are precluded from strengthening there when at the same time major policy areas toward the region from the United States are conducted by the Department of Defense rather than the Department of State, and especially when the U.S. Southern Command integrates U.S. civilian agencies under its leadership to coordinate policy toward Latin America.[28] The context for other emergent democracies, such as in southern Europe, was much more conducive to supporting civilian assertion. NATO and other Atlantic and European networks were very helpful in this regard in Spain, and later in east-central Europe, as other networks under the African Union may be in Africa and UN-led peacekeeping operations may be for Latin American and other countries. The crucial factor is that civilian democratic officials in governments and international organizations lead all these relations.[29]

THE POLICE

The security of citizens is an indispensable condition for the exercise and enjoyment of democratic rights. The forces that would provide that good have often proven weak in crime prevention and fighting and occasionally are found to have engaged in criminal acts themselves. For the most part, new democracies inherited police forces that were militarized or controlled by the military, abusive of human rights, sometimes corrupt, and nearly everywhere feared by the population. The paramount task in these cases was the demilitarization of the police force and its subjection to control by civilian democratic officials outside the defense sector.[30] A case in point was the transformation of Spain's Civil Guard—its demilitarization, its separation from the rest of the armed forces, and its subordination to the interior ministry—and the restructuring of the police to give way to a national police along with regional police forces in the 1970s.

Postconflict new democracies faced the much more complex challenge of creating new police services out of dismantled organizations, recruiting new personnel, and developing new organizational structures. Police became an indispensable part of the integral effort to develop administration and bureaucracy—a useable state.[31]

Establishing civilian leadership for the police and developing the appropriate institutional mechanisms for this leadership and control was neither easy nor fast. It often involved negotiations with actors from the previous regime or between organizations that were on opposite sides of armed conflict. Cases deemed successful, such as El Salvador or South Africa, moved persistently in the direction of reform with the support of political and social organizations and international organizations.

In many cases, however, government officials failed to devote enough attention to the forces of public order, choosing instead to concentrate on efforts to reform the military and redesign civil-military relations. This proved to be costly. Police forces enhanced their autonomy, opening up space for inefficiency and corruption to spread. Argentina, for instance, initially seen as a successful case of military reform, later reversed early gains and began considering use of the military for public order, given its inability to rein in a corrupt police force that had begun to resemble police in other places that elicited more fear from the population than did criminals.[32] Policing by the military has been done, in Latin America, in Brazil, Bolivia, Mexico, Peru, and El Salvador, and in numerous countries in other regions, including older democracies such as India. In Peru, behind the cover of a corrupt military clique under Fujimori, the police grew severely corrupt and inefficient. Even in the successful cases of El Salvador and South Africa, reorganized police forces (or services) were equally unable to prevent the rise in crime and insecurity. In El Salvador demilitarization took place before police reconstruction, giving rise to what was seen as a "demobilization dilemma."[33] This dilemma, especially in postconflict democracies, highlights both the interconnectedness of problems in the security sector and the need for simultaneity in advancing democratization and efficacy in security sector reform.

Failure to address early problems of police and citizen security often resulted in a growingly unmanageable police force precisely at a time of rising crime. This neglect was aided by a view that punishable crimes had more to do with the authoritarian past than with the realities of new democracies. Human rights organizations more used to censure than to working with government and the police also were, and in many places still are, very slow in adding issues of citizen security and police reform to their agendas.[34] In addition, government officials at times chose to ignore evidence of police abuse, including torture, under new democratic regimes, perhaps influenced by the idea that the latter almost by definition, and not through specific efforts and policies, would preclude such abuses.[35]

Lack of Effectiveness

Besides issues of demilitarization and control, democracies face in their police forces problems of sheer lack of effectiveness that are the result of major weaknesses in organization, equipment, training, methods, personnel policies, and recruitment. Of course, at the crux lie leadership problems that inhibit the pursuit of consistent and resolute policies that penalize behavior outside the rules, vigorously confront corruption, and secure political, public, and community support for reform and modernization.[36] A comprehensive and balanced approach would, for instance, resist pressures from media reports of rising crime that urge the adoption of "get tough" methods in policing or court procedures; these lose sight of the complexity of the problem and yield ineffective outcomes.

Organization

The critical organizational step of clearly delineating the chain of command is rarely taken, and proper coordination among units has left much to be desired. In some cases, special units developed to face specific crime problems stood outside that chain and became vulnerable to militarization.[37] Internal controls have not been set in place or have not functioned properly. Deployment of the force is not always responsive to actual crime trends, which is the result of poor or nonexistent research or of greater responsiveness to the needs of the wealthy and powerful than of the average citizen. Also, privatized or subcontracted security, expanding in many places, has not been subjected to police oversight in terms of procedures, outcomes, and impact over citizen's rights.[38]

Training

Training programs, especially in cases of new forces supported by international aid, have ceded to expediency, with specific demilitarized policing skills failing to develop fully. This results in use of excessive and unnecessary violence and, as in major Brazilian cities, very high death rates by police.[39] Training in the various methods to investigate and act on crime in ways that are compatible with citizens' rights but at the same time effective in crime reduction is usually poor.

Personnel and Recruitment

Personnel and recruitment problems have to do with the size of the force, which is usually smaller than needed, mostly because of scarce financing resources. The negative consequences of poor training are sometimes worsened by recruitment that does not always carefully screen to avoid reentry of abusive former state agents. But personnel problems also have to do with morale, proper payment, personnel policies, and rights. Personnel at the lower end of the organization, the one that actually does the policing, often ends up paying the price of leadership failures expressed in community mistrust. Policing as a critical part of a useable state demands that personnel receive the proper respect due all state employees. Internal controls for this purpose and the office of ombudsperson for police personnel have been used successfully to some degree in cases such as, recently, Peru.[40]

Transparency and Accountability

Principles and mechanisms that guarantee transparency, accountability, and solid connections with the community are indispensable in confronting these problems.[41] For instance, moderately successful attempts at legitimization by the new South African police service followed these principles by promoting local policing and accountability through community police fora and a number of other initiatives.[42] Also Brazil has been active in promoting police-community partnerships in some states and major cities as part of larger police reform efforts.[43] Improved performance, however, cannot advance without simultaneous implementation of justice sector reforms, including better prison system and reintegration policies. Indeed, police effectiveness in a manner compliant with democratic procedures may not really be advanced without parallel movements in other state institutions, political society, and civil society. And reformers must be cognizant of the possibilities and especially the limitations found in social and economic conditions expressed in large and increasing inequality gaps within societies, and other sources of division in society,[44] as well as the relentless and creeping action of international organized crime.[45]

INTELLIGENCE

Intelligence services are indispensable tools for informed decision making by democratic state officials in areas concerning internal and external security, especially in light of growing transborder threats including international organized crime and terrorism. New democracies have faced problems in this area that are not all that different from those of other state security sectors. Either the bulk of intelligence organization was inherited from previous regimes, and remained weak, underutilized, or strong and autonomous from new democratic officials, or it had to be recreated entirely. Recreation or reorganization has been generally slow, as this area requires a level of expertise that cannot be improvised. Following the concern with the transformation of civil-military relations and the police, intelligence came last.[46]

While the most politicized and repressive information services of previous authoritarian rulers were for the most part dismantled—albeit with little or no control of records, dossiers, and former agents—many other services, such as those in the armed forces and the police, remained in place. The ability to effectively control them has of course been dependent on the ability to actually establish civilian democratic control over the military, on which great variation is observed among new democracies. Generally, however, these are services that have resisted outside control. The first and quite challenging task of democratic governance here is establishing firm subordination, to legitimate democratic officials and to keep agencies specialized in foreign intelligence, such as those in the military, from venturing into domestic intelligence.

Leadership and Control

At different points after democratization the new regimes set out to create new agencies, such as South Africa's creation of the National Intelligence Agency in 1995 to replace the National Intelligence Service, or Chile's recent creation of the National Information Agency.[47] Also Brazil reorganized and civilianized its national intelligence during democratization, and Peru has debated the creation of a national system. While all this aims at enhancing state capacity in a critical area, strong separate intelligence services remain outside the control or actual scope of coordination of the new agencies.

Here again, a clear chain of command is essential for asserting a leadership that guarantees compliance with legally established rules as well as effectiveness in the task of producing relevant information. Control and leadership are, especially when it comes to intelligence, not established once and for all, and should be seen as a process. This is more the case in new democracies that will employ reconstructed segments of the intelligence capacity of the previous regimes. The result here will come from changes within those services to accommodate the new democratic situation and from new rules laid out by democratic authorities. Efforts should aim at strict compliance with the constitutional order and specific legislation over the intelligence service.

Accountability and Oversight

However, accountability and oversight are the most important features of setting up intelligence in democracy, beyond the fundamental necessity of control and government leadership to lay out mission and guidelines. A number of oversight models are offered to new democracies, ranging from congressional or parliamentary committees to special committees such as the generally praised Canadian Security Intelligence Review Committee, formed by privy councilors appointed by the governor, and who are not members of Parliament. Several features behind Canada's system have been highlighted as the basis for its impact, such as independence from the executive; the power to initiate inquiries; a membership that reflects the political spectrum but is not partisan in manner; extensive access to information; institutional expertise and adequate support staff; and the capacity to mobilize public opinion through the media.[48] The provision of expert staff for oversight committees, whether in Parliament or outside, is emphasized as required for the success of these committees, as is the integration and full use of oversight organizations in civil society.[49]

Danger of an "Intelligence State"

Although new democracies have had a hard time setting up or recreating intelligence services, old democracies face a no less daunting task with regard to leadership, control, and oversight of these services. In fact, because of their longer existence, extensive expertise, and bureaucratic complexity, those services have become talented at avoiding control, or not providing information requested by oversight bodies. During the current expansion of the use of these services internally to counter terrorist threats, failures of leadership and oversight have become more visible, influencing the quality of information and threatening long-held citizen freedoms and rights, raising what Philip Heymann has called "the problem of drifting into an 'Intelligence State.'"[50] The dangers of illegal means of obtaining information, including torture and the recent practice of rendition, are coupled with failures of processing and analysis of information, as reported, for instance, in the Iraq Study Group Report.[51] The search for effectiveness in organizing and reforming intelligence in new democracies should center in control and coordination, while allowing for varying degrees of decentralization, and stay clear of illegal means that undermine efforts at strengthening the rule of law and democratic institutions.

This brief review of the security sector problems new democracies struggle with has highlighted the different challenges they face according to the ways in which democracy was attained as well as the difficulties confronting old democracies in the new security context. The review has also shown the paths followed by cases of reform success and the major areas of concern facing those still in the effort to reform in order to attain both democratic control and effectiveness. Below some of the major conclusions of this review are presented in terms that may be useful as orientations for the future.

In the first place, policies must follow an integrated approach that views all elements of the security sector as essentially interrelated. However, an integrated and comprehensive approach should maintain strict separation among military, police, and intelligence functions and remain cognizant of its relation to developments in other state institutions, political society, and civil society.

The most essential ingredient of success in countering threats to democracy in this area is firmly established civilian leadership that is policy consistent and persistent and works through a clear chain of command. Developing central institutions, such as the establishment and empowerment of a civilian-led ministry of defense, is essential for materializing that leadership. Advisory councils for the top political leadership are useful instruments, but they should reflect that interrelatedness as well as primarily civilian political input from both political and civil society.

Internal controls as well as external accountability and oversight are indispensable for both effectiveness in performance and compliance with the rule of law. White papers and similar kinds of reports have been useful in generating healthy debates and conditions for the involvement of different actors in oversight. At the same time, institutions for executive leadership and control as well as those for oversight must develop expert civilian staff that allows for effective and continuous policy guidance and control. Institutions for research in this area both within and outside the public sector are necessary to support leadership, control, and oversight. Civil society organizations, including human rights organizations and think tanks, must be brought in for public debate of security issues and policies and for oversight functions.

Active participation and engagement in official international organizations helps affirm civilian political leadership and control over security sector agencies. Direct military-to-military relations or similar relations involving other agencies should be closely monitored. Military-led foreign relations and policies such as those from the U.S. Southern Command toward Latin America are generally detrimental.

Finally, the cultural context and the sets of values and attitudes that develop around the security sector and in society at large will play a critical role in the long run. Specific policies must be developed to address and counter value and attitude gaps between members of security sector agencies and society. Leadership and control over educational components in the security sector should be a priority, jointly with other means of bridging this gap. In cases where truth reports followed the establishment of democracy, useful guidelines were provided in the implementation recommendations, and these ought to be viewed as a resource for a continuous public debate that leads to reducing cultural gaps between security sectors and society.

CHAPTER FOUR

Beyond Threats to Democracy from the Armed Forces, Police, and Intelligence

The Spanish Case

NARCÍS SERRA

Seven policy questions guide my essay about the Spanish experience and its implications for democracies in danger.[1]

1. In the area of intelligence, how can democracies effectively defend themselves against international crime and terrorism, by their own actions and by new forms of cooperation with other democracies, in ways that are fully consistent with democratic values and practices?
2. Can the September 11, 2001, attacks in New York and the March 11, 2004, attacks in Madrid, and their aftermaths, shed any light on the interrelationship between democratic executives and legislatures and their management of the military, the police, and intelligence services?
3. Has the fight against international terrorism changed the use of the armed forces, in the classic sense of the term?
4. How can governments design and train police forces that are accessible to and trusted by their democratic citizens?
5. What could be considered the democratically optimal international coordination among the democracies concerning their police, intelligence, and military forces?
6. Can new efficacious arrangements be considered that are fully consistent with democratic values?

7. How is the European Union, within which Spain is a full and active participant, creating new institutions and procedures to increase the security of its citizens without diminishing any democratic freedoms?

The responses to these questions have great urgency not only for Spain but for many of the new democracies in danger. We are living at a time when many of the transition processes that could be included in the so-called Third Wave have reached a standstill or, at the very least, have taken a turn for the worse. These partially democratic states suffer from forms of military interventionism very different from the increasingly improbable coup d'état. Indeed, the Spanish case is a particularly interesting source for comparative policy studies because it is one of the few so far in which, in the areas of the democratic control, the military, police, and intelligence services, there has been nearly full consolidation of democratic procedures.

It is a well-accepted fact that threats from armies, police, and intelligence services to a democratic system appear in inverse proportion to the democratic maturity or consolidation of the country in question. It is also worth mentioning that the threat is greater if the above three forces are directly coordinated among themselves and, especially, when the three of them depend on the armed forces.

The Spanish case suggests that it is difficult for one of these forces to present problems in isolation and proves that reforms of all three services to make them democratic should not only be interlinked to ensure success but should also be part of a democratization process of the whole system.

Once a certain level of democratic consolidation has been achieved, the threats or problems that these three sectors may represent to the democratic system will be related to: (a) the use made by the executive of these sectors as part of the state administration; and (b) the tendency of the armed forces, and the other two sectors to a lesser extent, to extend and strengthen their autonomy—to act as institutions and not as part of the administration.

Spain is a good example of the new security framework and threats to it that have arisen since the end of the cold war and the onset of the current globalization process. It has many of the same problems, challenges, and needs as most of the other democratic countries, with the exception of the United States, which is on a completely different level because of its incomparable military strength.

SPANISH EXPERIENCE IN THE TRANSITION AND CONSOLIDATION PROCESSES

The Armed Forces

The armed forces were one of the most important factors in the Spanish transition process, although it is obvious that, unlike in other countries, they neither launched nor encouraged the authoritarian regime. It is true that the Franco regime may not be considered a military dictatorship in the strictest sense of the term, as the military forces did not hold power as a corporate body. But the armed forces were the final guarantors of the survival of Franco's regime; they had exclusive control of the forces of law and order, and the great majority identified fully with the ideological postulates of Franco. Moreover, when the dictator died, almost all of the political groups that supported the regime were dissolved, and the armed forces became the guarantors of the system's continuity. Declarations by top-ranking officers at the time prove that they believed this to be their mission. Admiral Pita da Veiga, navy minister during General Franco's final years and the first years of the monarchy until he resigned due to his opposition to the legalization of the Communist Party, declared in an official speech: "We oversee the security of the Homeland and ensure that its essence remains unaltered for we are its custodians."

It is obvious, from today's perspective, that the progressive consensus among political forces regarding the transition and the new Constitution, together with the widespread and proven popular support of the process led by Adolfo Suárez, to begin with, and then by the Socialist government under Felipe González from 1982, were key factors in the success of the military transition. However, there were other factors that should be taken into account as far as the process and the military are concerned. First of all, the King, Juan Carlos I, acknowledged by the military as the Caudillo's legitimate successor, was an essential point of reference for the armed forces coming to realize the need for sweeping political changes.

Secondly, the appointment of General Gutiérrez Mellado as deputy prime minister for defense issues opened up the way to necessary military reforms while at the same time preventing the formation of a corporate leadership to lead the armed forces in impeding change.

The process of gradual control over the armed forces can be divided into seven stages, although the stages do overlap some. These phases are well adapted to the Spanish case and provide elements of reflection for the majority of other cases.

In the first phase, there was more or less total control of political power by the armed forces or by the Francoist framework within which the military were fully involved. That was the situation throughout Franco's forty-year dictatorship.

In the second phase, immediately following the death of Franco, the armed forces had tutelage of the government, since they considered themselves guardians of the national essence and discussed the possibility of acting as a corporate body when they believed the situation required it. We can situate this phase in the first few months of the monarchy until Carlos Arias Navarro was replaced by Adolfo Suárez as prime minister and, possibly, including the first moments of Suarez's government until the appointment of General Gutiérrez Mellado.

In the third phase, the military had lost much of their power but still had the capacity, and occasionally used it, to condition government policy by limiting the reach of political reforms and/or by vetoing certain actions. Examples of such conditioning in this phase are: the meeting of the lieutenant generals of the three armed forces with the prime minister in September 1976, in which they requested guarantees that the Communist Party would not be legalized; the direct and indirect conditions regarding the wording of the Constitution in 1978; and the blocking of the Parliament's decision to grant amnesty to the military members of UMD (Unión Militar Democrática) in 1979 and 1980.

Those three phases usually constitute the period of transition in which the essential factor is the "extrication" or loss of power and intervention capacity of the armed forces in politics. In the Spanish case, the three phases coincide approximately with the UCD (Unión de Centro Democrático) government.

The fourth phase is that in which the military relinquished overall political intervention but moved on to defending their organizational and political autonomy. A particularly strong example of this was the military's resistance to the creation of a ministry of defense, which would be endowed with the leadership capacity for military policy. A major part of this entailed transferring the functions and budgets of the three previously existing military ministries to the general staff of each force and to the Council of Chiefs of Staff, as "the highest collegiate body in the military chain of command." This fourth phase was only completed after the 1984 reform of the National Defense Act (Ley de Defensa Nacional), nine years after the death of Franco and the start of the democratic transition.

The fifth phase was marked by a struggle revolving around the formal, albeit partial, acceptance of civilian supremacy. The military made declarations at variance with civilian authorities, disobeyed certain orders, or acted on their own initiative against the will of civilian authorities. In Spain, the actions of the military justice system, handing out minimum or no sentences for acts of insubordination against the civilian authorities and maximum sentences for certain actions by democratic members, is a good example of this struggle.

The sixth phase can be called the fight to maintain the ideological controls of the military as a whole. The military corporation accepted organizational controls but endeavored to maintain autonomous decisions on its professional definition, military training, access to a military career, and mechanisms for internal promotion. This sixth phase shares hazy borderlines with the seventh and final phase, which corresponds to the democratic control of the armed forces. At the end of the seventh phase, executive power defines military policy, the ministry directs military policy and exerts the control and leadership of the armed forces while legislative power controls the executive and the military, and military justice has become integrated within the justice system that, in democracy, has to be the only one. In Spain's case, this phase became a reality only in the last two years of the 1980s, almost thirteen years after the death of Franco and ten years after the ratification of the democratic Constitution.

The last four phases constitute the period of democratic consolidation, which, as far as the armed forces are concerned, implies that democratic power emerging in the transition went on to control and lead them. That was the task of the Socialist government after the 1982 elections.

Progress throughout the whole process was achieved by adopting measures coordinated on the following three axes both during the transition procedure and during consolidation:

1. The armed forces coming into line with the functioning and relations with executive and legislative power inherent to democratic countries. This implies ceding power and losing privileges and prerogatives.
2. The handling of the inevitable conflict, especially in the first phases of the process. This axis is often related to policy in general rather than to defense policy.
3. Professional redefinition, assimilation by the military of values closest to those of the society they serve, pushing the armed forces from being an institution that engages in contentious dialogue, or even a competing discourse, with the powers of state to becoming an integrated and loyal sector of the administration.

It is not easy to summarize the possible lessons to be learned from Spain about reducing possible threats from the military to maturing democracies in a few paragraphs. However, the first lesson should be the decisive influence of the progress of the general process of transition on the democratic-civilian control of the military. It is extremely difficult to create processes of democratic control of the military in semi-democracies or in democracies in danger without finding ways to foster the popular support for the government and undertaking reforms in other fields. In the Spanish case, military disputes increased in parallel to the weakness of Suárez's government and the decrease in its public support. The armed forces constitute the biggest threat to democracy during a transition process when overall progress toward democracy slows down or comes to a halt.

The creation and capacity building of a ministry of defense is key to the whole process. In Spain, Gutiérrez Mellado understood this lesson and eliminated the three previous ministries, following proposals drawn up with General Diaz Alegría in the final years of the dictatorship. This is true up to the point that the best and most comparable indicator of the degree of civilian control over the military achieved by a country is the analysis of its ministry of defense's true capacities.

The consolidation of democracy in this field is an evolutionary process from a completely institutional army that attempts to impose its values on society to armed forces that keep their own principles and values as requirements of their efficacy but participate in general in the values of their own society and the principles enshrined in the Constitution. Many aspects of the Spanish case helped in this process, ranging from legal reforms (military justice being made democratic) to the opening of the armed forces to women, and, crucially, the deep and detailed description of fundamental rights contained in the Constitution itself.

Spanish experience shows that it is not necessary that laws explicitly grant powers to the armed forces, because they attempt, in fact, to establish reserved domains of autonomy. It is enough for legislation to be ambiguous in that area. That is why any legislation limiting military autonomy should be very clear and explicit.

Finally, the elected democratic government's active and willing acceptance of the need to take control of military policy is a key factor for success in the whole process.

The Police

The police force was another institution in need of radical reform following the demise of the dictatorship, due to the eminently repressive and political character of police forces during that regime. Spain's fledgling democracy faced serious difficulties with the police. The police were basically loyal to the dictatorship and were controlled by the military because the Public Order Forces, the name given to the Armed Police and the Civil Guard (Policía Armada y Guardia Civil), were part of the armed forces, alongside the army, navy, and air force. Another difficulty was the need to maintain certain structures to fight ETA, the Basque separatist terrorist group.

The aim was clear right from the beginning; to gradually transform a markedly repressive police force, with institutions, for example, such as the Politico-Social Brigade, which was responsible for monitoring and controlling all the activities of the political and trade union opposition and frequently taking their leaders before the Public Order Tribunal, into a police force whose aim would be to guarantee law and order and to preserve individual rights and freedoms. But it was hard to get the security forces to act in accordance with the new situation; between 1975 and 1978 they caused the death of twenty-seven people when they intervened to dissolve demonstrations.

The Public Order Tribunal was dissolved prior to the passing of the Constitution, and in 1978 a new Police Act was approved. This legislation ended the repressive character of the police function and refocused the work of the police forces on numerous other tasks. A new force, the National Police Force, was created to replace the Armed Police, and any actions against the security forces were no longer judged by military tribunals, although the new police were not fully demilitarized because of tensions existing with the military.

The reforms were carried out to transform the image of the police. This included changing the gray uniform of the Armed Police, who were known as the "grays" (*los grises*), to brown. It is strange that brown was chosen when police officers were still considered members of the military, because army uniforms were also brown. In fact, the color had to be changed again later to navy blue.

The 1978 Constitution, in Article 104, explicitly ratified the spirit of many of these changes by describing the main mission of the Security Forces (the police and the Civil Guard) as "protecting the free exercise of rights and freedoms to guarantee law and order," thus eliminating any reference to the concept of "public order" so synonymous with the previous regime.

The most important decision made by the authors of the Constitution was to definitively separate the police and the Civil Guard from the armed forces. This was one of the most controversial issues in the debates on the text of the Constitution. The Alianza Popular members of Parliament and the military senators supported the maintenance of the police and Civil Guard within the armed forces right to the bitter end.

Implementing the principle was no easy feat either. The Constitution was not enough: even by 1980, several captain generals still claimed that military jurisdiction was competent for crimes committed by the National Police. An urgent reform of the Military Justice Code in 1980 in order to apply the Constitution on this point became necessary. Moreover, all police and Civil Guard commanders above a certain level were members of the military; otherwise they were obliged to study for two years at a military academy.

The right to join a trade union, freedom of assembly, and freedom of expression for members of police forces so that the police have the same rights as other citizens goes hand in hand with demilitarization. Legalizing police trade unions went a long way toward creating a new mentality in democratic Spain.

A second important measure already called for in the Constitution was the establishment of several different police forces, as the autonomous communities or regions were permitted to have their own. The Basque Country, Navarre, and Catalonia have since set up their own police forces.

A third important measure was the constitutional foresight of creating the judicial police at the orders of the examining judges. This was a clear innovation. Some scholars insist that a whole new judicial corps, distinct from the general corps, should have been established for those tasks, but that step is unnecessary as long as there are sufficient human and material resources and the regulations are clear and unambiguous.

Proof of the difficulties suffered by the Spanish transition in the field of the security forces was that the Organic State Security Forces Act (LOFCS) was not passed until 1986. That act definitively demilitarized the National Police and introduced the possibility of a civilian director general of the Civil Guard.

That act, together with the Civil Defense Act of 1985, have been criticized for their excessive centralism, for reserving that subject as being exclusive to the state, for creating inefficient cooperation, and for treating police forces in their organic sense, without contemplating an operational nature. The controversial 1992 Law and Order Act did pay more attention to those aspects and had to be amended after the Constitutional Court declared some of the powers granted to the Security Forces to be unconstitutional. Shortly after that, a long crisis started in the whole security sector that culminated in the flight of the first civilian director general of the Civil Guard after he used reserved/discretionary funds for his own personal benefit. Later on, the courts also sentenced other officials of the Ministry of Interior for the same reason.

The adaptation of Spanish police forces to the new political situation enables us to examine at least two further aspects of that democratic process, which in my judgment were not a complete success. The Ministry of Interior and the Ministry of Justice were merged. However, the Spanish experience does not endorse that measure as a solution to the inevitable problems of coordination, or even disputes, arising between the two. It is better to approach them as two fields that should be different, justice and national security, than to believe that merging both into one ministry can solve all problems. We should also remember that, without reducing the direct responsibility of the executive, the ultimate controllers of the police and their possible excesses are the judges. In retrospect, it cannot be said that in the Spanish case merging the two ministries contributed to increasing the efficacy of the security system.

The second problem area concerns reserved/discretionary funds. In Spain, both the Ministry of Defense, for the intelligence service, and the Ministry of Interior are endowed with reserved funds. The Spanish experience shows that it is essential to find mechanisms to control the use of those funds without eliminating their reserved conditions but involving Parliament. When the funds are controlled only by those who use them, there is almost an irresistible urge to use them, in the best of cases, unwisely, and in the worst, to the benefit of those who have access to them. This was a very significant factor in the security crisis in the final years of the Socialist government, when it was the cause of the flight and subsequent conviction of the first civilian director general of the Civil Guard and the origin of other legal proceedings against other Ministry of Interior officials.

In conclusion, we should consider the destabilizing potential for a democracy caused by crises in the state security apparatus. The crisis that occurred in Spain between 1994 and 1996, and that had a direct impact on the Civil Guard, the National Police Force, and the CESID (the Spanish Intelligence Agency), was the most serious shock to Spanish democracy since the attempted coup on February 23, 1981. The crisis was stoked by the opposition parties, prepared to stop at nothing to prevent the Socialist Party from continuing in government after four consecutive election victories. They even broke the State Antiterrorism Pact, but Spain's democratic system managed to resist the crisis and solved it by bringing a different party into power.

The Intelligence Services

At the time of Franco's death, apart from the police intelligence service devoted to the detection and dissolution of sectors opposed to the regime (the BIS, Brigade for Social Investigation), there were three more intelligence services: (1) the Higher Defense Staff, linked to the prime minister; (2) the Army Chief of Staff; and (3) the SECED (the intelligence service linked to the military and created in Franco's period), set up by Admiral Carrero Blanco, Franco's first prime minister, appointed toward the end of Franco's dictatorship and assassinated by ETA in 1973, to ascertain and counteract insubordination movements, especially in universities following the protests of 1968. The common denominator of all four of these intelligence services was that they were controlled by the military.

Despite its origins, and the fact that the first director of the SECED was involved in the coup of February 23 and even convicted for his role in it, the service did not openly fight the transition process. On the contrary, the SECED authorities played a decisive role in 1976 and 1977 by facilitating contacts between Adolfo Suárez's government and the democratic opposition in order to smooth the way to reforms, attempting to favor forces it considered more moderate than the Communist Party. They also participated, upon Adolfo Suárez's orders, in processes such as the dialogue with the president of the Generalitat de Catalunya (the Catalan regional government) in exile, Josep Tarradellas.

However, it was obvious that this body could not continue to exist in a democratic situation, and when General Gutiérrez Mellado was appointed, the government decided to merge the intelligence service of the High Defense Staff and the SECED, creating the CESID in 1978. This new service was part of the Ministry of Defense. In its first few years it lacked a clear mandate and effective government control and also suffered the inertias inherent to the activity its members had developed under the previous regime. It became obvious that a change in direction was absolutely necessary following the attempted coup in February 1981.

The government appointed Lieutenant Colonel Emilio Alonso Manglano as the CESID's director, opening up a radically different period during which the CESID provided valuable services by giving information on the internal situation within the armed offices, beginning with deactivating a further coup plan prepared for the eve of the elections in October 1982. The CESID carried out an activity, the struggle against involution, that no other institution could have handled as effectively.

After 1985 the fight against involution was no longer an absolute priority, and the CESID endeavored to become an intelligence service along the lines of those of democratic countries with which it cooperated, by boosting deployment abroad and granting priority to fighting terrorism. In December 1985 a decree replaced the ministerial order that had regulated the structure and missions of the CESID since September 1982. That decree paved the way for a new phase that culminated in a 2002 act creating the CNI (Centro Nacional de Inteligencia) to replace the CESID.

The Ministry of Interior tried to set up another intelligence service over the same period of time with a very solid pretext—the fight against terrorism—even forming a network abroad. Coordination between these services and those of the Civil Guard was always difficult, with obvious cases of missing investigation possibilities because one service or another would claim the leading role to the detriment of the others. Islamic terrorist attacks have proved that these coordination issues exist in almost all countries, and many have introduced reorganization processes within the executive or are in the midst of them. The existence of a certain plurality of services, however, would seem advisable, and an increase in parliamentary scrutiny encourages coordination within the Spanish government.

Indeed, the lessons to be learned from that era in Spain indicate that it is better to have a certain plurality of intelligence services even though this requires constant coordination efforts, which will differ depending on how threats evolve. One single service linked directly to the prime minister does not appear to be advisable because it cancels out the existence of a fusible dependence on a ministry, which is a necessity, as proven by the crisis of the national security forces as well as that of the CESID in the nineties.

Domestic intelligence services should be drastically reduced in size, and political intervention is necessary to break with the inertia of previous eras. Finally, the military must be limited to intelligence services in their own field, which requires embarking on a long "civilization" process. In Spain's case, NATO membership helped to define the intelligence tasks befitting each of the armed forces.

DEMOCRATIC STRUCTURES AND VALUES IN THE ERA OF GLOBALIZATION: THE NEW AGENDA

The Armed Forces in the Twenty-first Century: New Missions

Just as we may consider that the Spanish transition provides us with useful reflections on threats from the armed forces, the police, and the intelligence services, the Spanish case may also provide food for thought regarding the radical changes called for by globalization and the transformation of threats.

The terrorist attack of March 11, 2004, in Madrid was dramatic proof that Spain's concept of security needs to change: no neighboring state is threatening Spain's territorial integrity, but a huge number of citizens suffered a direct, brutal aggression in the commuter trains of Madrid. The relevant security threat is no longer "territorial," it is "human security." The United Nations has defined and fostered the concept of human security for the last ten years. Some countries, such as Canada, have adopted it, but it is very significant that the Organization of American States has also done so since its 2000 assembly, pursuing since then the formulation of the multidimensional nature of its concept of security so that the military instrument ceases to monopolize those problems.

The European Union approved its first security strategy in 2003. It includes plans for addressing threats such as terrorism, organized crime, states in decline, and regional conflicts. They are not European conflicts but global ones. But the really crucial issue is that not only have those organizations changed their perceptions and concepts, Spanish and world public opinion has too. In this sense, the European Security Strategy concluded that these threats cannot be tackled by purely military means and that each requires a mixture of instruments.

In this situation, problems with the armed forces may come mainly from their failure to adapt to new needs. In the Spanish case, public opinion considers spending money on armies to be unjustified because it believes that traditional missions no longer make sense. Getting the armed forces to fit into a democratic, administrative structure requires further effort than its subordination to civilian power; there is the need to find and make explicit their raisons d'être in current circumstances, preventing the military from searching for new missions within the country. It has been evident that the drastic reduction of the military budgets in most countries, above all in Eastern Europe and Latin America, is not a satisfactory solution by itself, even though it can reduce the conflicts between countries and help to finance social programs. The so-called Security Sector Reform is a necessity, above all in those countries where there has been a reduction of the armed forces capacities. Otherwise, the risk of debilitating the state and defining inadequate missions may increase.

In Spain the armed forces have not shown the tendency to look for new missions within the country because NATO and, specifically, EU membership, together with participation in numerous UN peacekeeping missions, imply continuous missions. There is no doubt that the progressive commitment of Spain's armed forces in UN peacekeeping missions has improved their image vis-à-vis Spanish public opinion, although it has come at a high price, such as the May 2003 air crash in Turkey in which sixty-two Spanish soldiers died. The use of the armed forces to contribute to the security of Spain through contributing to global security will depend on a Europe that is capable of achieving a multilateral and joint response to the new situation. In fact, to act at European level is much more efficient to contribute to global security than the sum of individual actions of all European nations.

Using the Spanish armed forces on foreign missions has helped prevent their use as an instrument against the terrorism of ETA, which would have been a serious danger. All of Spain's democratic governments have agreed on this point. It is essential to reduce social support for terrorism, and the use of the armed forces in Spain would be counterproductive because the terrorists could allege that they are at war with Spain, which is precisely what they want. In this sense, President Bush's declaration that the United States is at war with terror concedes, in fact, a first victory to the terrorists.

The new situation also questions the issue of military values and their distance from the values upheld by society. Today, it is hard to envision the Spanish armed forces used in battles against other armies in which the only aim is military victory. More realistic are operations in which the aim is to protect people, to separate warring factions, and/or to cooperate in peacekeeping while institutions are rebuilt in a region or in a country. To be efficacious in those fields requires sharing the principles and values that have led a society to undertake this type of activity. For this reason, the natural tendency of the armed forces to define their characteristics, their values, and the formation and training of their members in a corporate fashion must be counteracted. It is important for democratic leaders to understand that in our times, neither the definition of military values nor the definition of military doctrines can be an exclusively military task.

The strategic defense review approved recently in Spain echoes that situation, as it defines only three main missions for the armed forces: first, preventing any kind of aggression and, if necessary, responding to it; second, contributing to international peace and stability; and third, preserving the security and well-being of citizens, occasionally contributing to tasks of civilian administration when appropriate. Those definitions were drawn up by consensus among the most significant political parties in 2003.

The current Spanish experience suggests four lines of work with regard to the armed forces in countries that cannot yet be considered fully consolidated democracies. They are:

- Define new missions for the armed forces, especially in the areas of human security and international collaboration. This definition will help prevent the armed forces from attempting to cover any perceived legitimacy deficit that would entail the mere continuity of traditional missions, or the seeking out of new domestic missions, which might imply unacceptable interventionism in the state or displace the civilian administration from its own tasks.
- Continue with the modernization of the security and defense sector, establishing ministries of defense equivalent to those existing in already consolidated democracies.
- Foster mechanisms of regional cooperation in the field of security, as the European process has been essential to solving problems in Spain.
- Guide and direct the armed forces of each country toward a progressive contribution to regional and international governance.

The Police as a Public Service

In the time elapsed since the end of the dictatorship in Spain, we may say that a complete change in mentality has occurred, both in members of the police force as well as in the general public. The police have gone from being an institution at the service of the state to a force at the service of citizens. Because of this, rather than talking about the necessary reforms to prevent it being a threat to democracy, it is more fitting to analyze the changes that can lead to greater efficacy and respond to new challenges to domestic security. It may also be stated that the serious terrorist threat of ETA, until very recently has slowed willingness to introduce reforms by an executive that was concerned by the possible loss of efficacy during the change process. There is, in fact, consensus that the police reforms need to have major parliamentary support, both because it is question of state legitimacy and because a stable framework is a prerequisite for police efficacy.

The most pressing issues for reform currently are linked to new threats and risks involved in globalization. We need to mention international terrorism but also drug trafficking, organized mafias, and the possible control of immigration flows.

Secondly, we should also mention that coordination among the different police forces is an unresolved issue so far. The Constitution established a police system on three levels: the state police, the regional (autonomous community) police, and the local or municipal police. They were intended to be coordinated by security committees at different levels, but in reality those mechanisms only solve some problems of policy coordination. Operational cooperation is insufficient, beginning with the state level, between the National Police Force and the Civil Guard. The new threats brought by globalization require an urgent increase in police coordination. There are opinions in favor of merging the police and the Civil Guard, terminating the latter's military condition, as the safest way to guarantee coordinated action. However, at the same time, the new international situation has revealed the advantages of a militarized police corps, which may be the best adapted to most international missions. A first step forward has been the merger of the director general of police and the director general of Civil Guard into a single post in September 2006.

The Spanish Ministry of Foreign Affairs announced at the UN Security Council that Spain is going to create a special thousand-strong Civil Guard unit devoted to international missions. That decision is linked to other European countries (France, Italy, Portugal, and Holland) that have decided to set up a European Gendarmerie Force capable of deploying eight hundred police within one month. Based in Vincenza (Italy), this force was officially inaugurated on January, 23, 2006.

Third, there is a need for reforms to contribute to improved efficacy of the whole system of law and order. One of the most urgent tasks is to boost local police forces, especially in big cities, as their greater proximity to the public makes them more efficient at combating and preventing urban crime. They should be able to act as judicial police, at least with regard to petty crime. That would require legal reforms, fostering local justice and quick trials. Spain has more police than the European average, so it is not a question of increasing manpower but rather of reallocating functions and putting an end to the scant importance current legislation accords municipal police forces.

Fourth, Spain needs to undertake the reforms necessary to bring itself into line with all the efforts being made within the European Union against organized crime and terrorism, compatible with the creation of closer cooperation mechanisms with its neighbors Portugal and France.

In recent years, and after September 11, 2001, the EU has adopted different measures to improve European cooperation in the fight against terrorism, such as the creation of the law enforcement agency Eurojust, joint investigation teams, and the European arrest warrant. At the same time, Europol has been endowed with new functions in the fight against terrorism, and new legislation has been adopted with regard to financing terrorism and laundering money. However, many of these new institutions are not yet fully functioning, and many of the adopted measures have not been implemented. After the attacks of March 11, 2004, in Madrid, the EU gave a new impetus to antiterrorist policies by creating the post of EU counterterrorism coordinator. This post has the responsibility to improve the coordination among all of the EU countries to ensure that the measures approved since 2001 are truly implemented. The first EU counterterrorism coordinator, the Dutch Gijs de Vries, was appointed in 2004. Three years later he resigned, claiming personal reasons. He had been unable to make his mark in the job due to difficulties working with the European National Ministries of Home Affairs. After his resignation, the development of this policy was practically paralyzed for six months until the designation of the Belgian Gilles de Kerchove d'Ousselghem as the new EU counterterrorism coordinator.

The European Council of December 2005 approved the European Union Counterterrorism Strategy. The EU understands that the fight against terrorism has to be based in the respect for human rights as well as to allow European citizens to live in freedom, security, and justice. The strategy envisages different measures to achieve four broad objectives: prevent, protect, pursue, and respond.

The comparison between the EU strategy and the U.S. national strategy for combating terrorism is unavoidable. One of the main differences between the two is the emphasis within the EU on police and judicial capacities, while the United States focuses more on military capacities. In this sense, the European Union has made more progress than the United States in the field of police, judicial, and intelligence services cooperation. Another important difference is the European strategy's emphasis on the prevention of terrorism. The European Union seeks to combat radicalization and recruitment into terrorism through integration, equality of opportunity, respect for human rights, and the rule of law. That is to say, the EU seeks to combat terrorism from its roots, not only to fight against terrorist attacks. In sum, the European countries have developed their own approach to fight terrorism, different from the American one and always respecting human rights and the rule of law.

The Intelligence Services and New Challenges to Security

New threats, and specifically international terrorism, have shown the need for radical changes to boost intelligence services. During the cold war, apart from the difficulties in obtaining relevant intelligence about the Soviet Union, we trusted in the United States' intelligence just as we trusted in its capacity for military response. That can no longer be the case when threats come from within the country, as the Atocha train bombings dramatically proved. Events have also proven that Islamic terrorism depends on connections to networks of common criminals to carry out its actions (for example to buy explosives) and to finance them. Relevant information to prevent and combat common crimes, perpetrated by organized gangs or not, should be matched with information that, so far, has been the domain of intelligence services devoted to monitoring foreign countries.

Nor can we continue to rely exclusively upon the intelligence of one single country, no matter how strong it is. The new situation means increasing intelligence capacity in each country and intense cooperation among nations. Clues to the authors of the March 11 train bombings, just like those of September 11, 2001, were found in several countries, and the network was only fully revealed after a pooling, no holds barred, of information from different domestic and foreign national services.

In these circumstances, the new Spanish laws ought to confront three issues that tend to be common problems in the intelligence services: dependence (who do they receive orders from?), coordination, and control. The law does not introduce any changes as far as dependence is concerned, although it does permit this to be changed by decree. That seems reasonable, since the Ministry of Foreign Affairs does not seem suited to this complex new dimension of intelligence, and locating the service within the Ministry of Interior would entail concentrating three very powerful services there; the police, the Civil Guard, and the CNI. Spanish experience shows that the existence of counterweights has been a necessary, albeit insufficient, factor in the control of intelligence services.

The 2002 act created a government delegate committee, chaired by one of the deputy prime ministers, for the coordination issue. The risk of that solution is similar to that mentioned with regard to police coordination: policy cooperation moves forward but does not necessarily imply an improvement in operational coordination. That is the great unresolved issue in this area.

Finally, the law introduces a highly suitable innovation at a time when it is worth remembering, permanently at that, that the fight against terrorism should be fought following lines and principles always acceptable in a democracy. A Supreme Court judge is appointed for a five-year period with the mission of ensuring that intelligence service operations require judicial authorization when they may affect citizens' rights.

The evolution of Spain's security systems, as well as the radical transformation of the concept of security in recent years, provides thought-provoking material regarding this sector.

First of all, it should be stated that the new situation increases the risk of the information services being used to justify policies decided by the government or attitudes that favor party politics rather than the national interest, as has occurred in the United States and Great Britain. In Spain, the attempt to maintain ETA as the perpetrator of the Atocha bombings in the belief that it would benefit the party in government in the general election led to an election turnaround in precisely the opposite direction. Greater parliamentary control may avoid or offset that type of attitude in the future. The drastic specialization of services, distinguishing foreign from domestic, may be of limited functionality in current circumstances. The demilitarization of intelligence services is advisable not just for reasons of democratic consolidation but also for efficacy, given the decrease in purely military threats.

Spain is facing these new challenges having learned the lesson that the battle against terrorism must be fought with all the arms of the rule of law. Although not all terrorism is the same, to say the least, acting in consequence with this principle is an indispensable prerequisite in the efficacy of the fight; the reduction of the threat of terrorism always means reducing social support for it. For this very reason, the use of acceptable means in a democratic state is a necessary ingredient for success. In Spain, issues such as the deaths of alleged terrorists in police custody and the existence of the GAL (death squads illegally set up by officials of the Spanish Government to fight ETA) and other illegal state-created antiterror organizations in different guises, for example, only served to increase ballot box support for ETA-sympathizing organizations and, in fact, delayed the reduction of that terrorist threat.

At the end of this analysis, which has covered the armed forces, police, and intelligence services at the same time, we may consider that the fight against terrorism will probably not require the use of the armed forces, in the classic sense of the term, in the near future. The burden of that fight will reside in the political, police, and information-services domains.

The greatest danger in the military domain lies in the difficulty of using the armed forces without creating, de jure or de facto, a situation inherent to war that justifies extremisms in public opinion. War is used to support illegalities such as Guantánamo, the instructions issued at Abu Ghraib prison, or bombing rebels and killing untold numbers of civilians in the process. War is also used to justify fighting with any means—kidnapping, beheading civilians, or indiscriminate car-bomb attacks.

If the aim is to overthrow tyrants and promote progress toward democracy, we should conclude that such tactics are completely wrong direction to take. The Spanish experience, although highly specific, is unequivocal. Democracy emerges strengthened when moderate public opinion is strengthened and is weakened in the face of public support for extreme positions.

It is necessary to effectively attack the causes that produce or nurture terrorism within the political realm. It should be considered a matter of "hearts and minds" if we truly wish to move toward stable solutions. The police sphere will require a quick effort at adaptation to the new threats and a redefinition of tasks, for example with the local police forces that would respond to the risks associated with current interdependence. The intelligence services field must also radically change its priorities. It must move from monitoring states to organized gangs, terrorist or otherwise, and seek the mechanisms for international cooperation so necessary today, even if it entails losing sovereignty. The citizens prefer security to sovereignty. They may feel in the medium term that the state is powerless against those security issues, and this can also cause disaffection for a system of freedoms. Preventing this risk has to be the objective of the European political project rather than the aim of national authorities.

PART THREE

Refining Presidentialism and Semi-presidentialism

CHAPTER FIVE

Latin America's Interrupted Presidencies

Alternatives?

ARTURO VALENZUELA

Over a quarter of a century has passed since Latin America began what has turned out to be the fullest and most enduring experience it has ever had with constitutional democracy. While dictatorships were the norm in the 1960s and 1970s—only Colombia, Costa Rica, and Venezuela avoided authoritarian rule during those decades—today an elected government rules in every Latin American country except Cuba. As David Scott Palmer notes, between 1930 and 1980, the twenty countries that make up Latin America underwent 277 changes of government, 104 of which (or 37.5 percent) took place via military coup. From 1980 to 1990, by contrast, only seven of the thirty-seven changes of government in the region took place through military interventions, just two of which can be fairly described as clearly antidemocratic in intent. The overall number of coups was the lowest for any single decade in Latin American history since independence in the early nineteenth century.[1]

The coups of the 1980s were confined to just four countries: Bolivia, Haiti, Guatemala, and Paraguay. Since 1990, only Haiti and Peru have seen elected constitutional governments successfully replaced by force. In 1989, Argentines witnessed their country's first transfer of power from one civilian chief executive to another in more than sixty years. In 2000, Mexico marked its emergence as a multiparty democracy after more than seven decades of one-party rule. Most Latin American states have never had so many successive elected governments come to power without authoritarian reversals.[2]

Nonetheless, the euphoria that accompanied democracy's rise has waned. Opinion polls show that Latin Americans still broadly support democracy and prefer it to dictatorship by a better than four-to-one margin. Yet the same surveys reveal a growing dissatisfaction with democracy and a readiness to question the benefits and the performance of democratic governments.[3]

Particularly troubling is a continuing pattern of instability that affects governance at the highest levels. In country after country, presidents have seen their job-approval ratings plummet, while those of legislators and party leaders have tumbled even more steeply. Many a president has left office trailing dashed hopes and enfeebled institutions, but at least has left according to schedule. Fifteen presidents, however, have not. This group has suffered the indignity of early removal through impeachment or forced resignation, sometimes under circumstances of instability that have threatened constitutional democracy itself. A sixteenth chief executive interrupted the constitutional order by closing congress.

In the past, the military was at the heart of the problem. Ambition-driven generals might eject an elected president from office or bar the implementation of policies that the soldiers and their allies did not like. New figures and forces might gain admission to the military-run "game" of politics if they took care not to advocate anything that sounded too radical or populist. Officers would arbitrate among factions and decide when to call for new elections to restore civilian rule, and coups in turn always enjoyed the complicity of civilian elites.[4] After Fidel Castro seized power in Cuba and set up a revolutionary-communist regime on the island in 1959, polarization intensified throughout the region, and military juntas increasingly began to leave behind political refereeing in favor of full-blown "bureaucratic-authoritarian" dictatorship.[5]

Latin American democracy no longer faces threats from United States–supported local elites that fear any reform movement as a possible Soviet front. Military governments failed overwhelmingly to cope with the economic and social crises of the 1970s and 1980s. Toward the end of that period, U.S. foreign policy reacted to the winding down of the cold war by shifting from support for authoritarian regimes as necessary if distasteful bulwarks against communism to recognition that authoritarianism was thwarting the consolidation of legitimate governments. The United States joined other nations of the Western Hemisphere in creating mechanisms to stop any forcible disruptions of constitutional democracy.[6] In what has been a sea change since the cold war, Latin American militaries no longer mix openly in politics.

FAILED PRESIDENCIES

Decreased polarization and the military's withdrawal to the barracks did not, however, usher in an era of uniformly successful presidential governments. Instability remains a persistent problem and sometimes proceeds along lines that are eerily reminiscent of the unhappy past. For two decades—from Bolivian president Hernán Siles Suazo's 1985 abandonment of office amid hyperinflation to Ecuadorean president Lucio Gutiérrez's early departure in 2005—a lengthy list of presidents failed to complete their constitutionally prescribed terms (for a complete listing of these "interrupted" chief executives, see the chapter appendix).

Three cases differ enough from the others to merit special mention. In Haiti, Aristide was actually toppled twice. The first coup against him came in September 1991, nine months after he had won a resounding victory in a December 1990 popular election. This was a "classic" military putsch carried out with strong support from a tiny civilian elite fearful of the former radical priest's populism. Restored after an October 1994 U.S. military intervention, Aristide hung on through a nonconsecutive second term that began in 2001 while the overwhelming problems of his country (the Western Hemisphere's poorest) festered. They continued to do so even after brigand gangs and disgruntled ex-soldiers descended on Port-au-Prince and forced him—under disputed circumstances—to flee in a U.S.-furnished plane to the Central African Republic on February 29, 2004.

In Peru, President Alberto Fujimori (a political outsider who had won a runoff election after garnering just 25 percent of the vote in the November 1990 first round) executed an *autogolpe* (self-coup). Chafing at the prospect of having to cut deals with a legislature dominated by his foes, he recruited military support and shuttered Congress in April 1992. International condemnation was swift and widespread, but Fujimori's decisive actions (including victories over the Shining Path terrorist movement) helped him to secure both congressional-election victories for his allies and his own reelection to a second term in 1995. Fujimori was forced to step down in 2000 amid controversy over an openly flawed election as he sought a third term in office.

The third unusual case involves the Dominican Republic, where the decision to cut short the final term of longtime president Joaquín Balaguer came before his actual inauguration. In 1994, the aged Balaguer had won a sixth term by a tiny margin, edging out an old rival in a bitter race marked by widespread fraud charges and continuing civil unrest. Acting under the strong coaxing of the U.S. State Department, Balaguer helped to defuse the situation by letting his term be cut from five years to two and agreeing never to run again.

In the remaining thirteen cases, each president left office early amid severe economic, political, and social turmoil that the president's own immediate departure was widely seen as essential to resolving. Some presidents found themselves forced out after they took actions deliberately intended to suspend or undermine democracy. Others found that their position faced erosion not only due to flagging public confidence and surging unrest but also because military leaders could no longer guarantee order and support. A final group left under less dramatic circumstances that came down to abysmal performance and nose-diving public support.

On May 25, 1993, Guatemala's President Jorge Serrano tried to break a perceived stalemate with the 116-member legislature (in which his party held only eighteen seats) by means of a Fujimori-style self-coup. He arrested congressional leaders, Supreme Court judges, and the national ombudsman, and then announced elections for a constituent assembly to be held within six months. It all soon went sour, however, as the international community, party leaders, business groups, the armed forces, and thousands of student and civic-group demonstrators lined up against him. On June 1, senior officers who had been in touch with the opposition told Serrano that he and his supportive vice president would have to go. Congress chose the former human rights ombudsman to fill the presidency.

In Ecuador seven years later, it was also high-ranking soldiers who pressured President Jamil Mahuad out of office after indigenous protestors and rebellious troops occupied Congress to show their anger at the austerity measures that he had proposed to deal with economic stagnation and a ballooning deficit. Mahuad's ouster was part of the deal that the high command made in order to end the takeover. Mahuad, who had garnered only 35 percent in the first round of the 1998 presidential race, and whose party held only 35 out of 121 congressional seats, had lurched from crisis to crisis with scant support. He met the same fate as his predecessor, Abdala Bucaram, and as his successor Lucio Gutierrez.

Another failed president turned out to be the twice-elected Fujimori. Riding his early successes in fighting terrorism and boosting Peru's economy, the former agronomics professor leaned heavily on military and secret-police allies and never bothered much with serious party building or congressional relations. After his 1995 reelection, he began pressing the courts for a constitutional interpretation that would allow him to run for a third term. His public support waned and his hard-line, autocratic style caught up with him when his efforts to rig the April 2000 election sparked mass protests and strong international condemnation. Facing likely impeachment and criminal charges after his spy chief was caught offering bribes, Fujimori went to Japan and sent in his resignation in November 2000. Congress passed over his vice president and chose its own presiding officer as temporary chief executive pending fresh balloting.

Bolivia's Siles Suazo had been his country's president from 1956 to 1960. He returned to office in 1982 after years of coups and countercoups, only to face massive economic problems including hyperinflation. With no majority in either house of Congress and a fiercely restive labor movement on his hands, he saw his economic-stabilization policies repeatedly collapse as he strove in vain to bridge the gap between the standards set by the International Monetary Fund (IMF) and the demands of domestic groups. Nothing seemed to work. Rule by decree, efforts to lobby Congress, and the appointment of a technocratic cabinet proved similarly fruitless as the indecisive Siles Suazo wavered from one approach to another, finally resorting to a hunger strike as a desperate way to gain public sympathy. With his support crumbling and coup rumors abounding, the president at last agreed to a Catholic Church–brokered agreement under which Congress moved the presidential election forward by a year, cutting his mandate short.

In 1989, observers of Brazilian politics were surprised when an obscure provincial governor named Fernando Collor de Mello managed to parlay charm, good looks, and a media-savvy "antipolitics" message into 28.5 percent of the first-round vote and an eventual presidential runoff win. Collor, whose ad hoc party held just 5 percent of the seats in Congress, soon alienated the older parties. Congressional efforts to limit his powers, plus a faltering, inflation-wracked economy, forced him to move grudgingly toward expanding his legislative coalition. Before he got very far, however, a corruption scandal brought about his impeachment and resignation in 1992.

Venezuela's Carlos Andres Pérez (1989–93) was exceptional in that both he and his party had won electoral majorities. Pérez had overseen a strong economy during a previous turn as president in the late 1970s, and people reeling from the effects of declining oil prices on the petroleum-dependent Venezuelan economy hoped that he would turn things around. Facing soaring budget deficits and inflationary pressures, Pérez moved swiftly to implement an IMF-approved austerity package that included fuel-price hikes. The result was unrest violent and widespread enough to drive Pérez to declare martial law. His governing style did not help him win support for his policies even among his own partisans. His own party's leaders, many of whom had resisted his candidacy, resented him for not adequately informing them of his initiatives and for ignoring their reform proposals. In October 1991, Pérez lost ground in internal party elections. The year following, two unprecedented military uprisings (army colonel and future president Hugo Chávez led the first) left 120 people dead. As Pérez's own party abandoned him amid charges that he had misused secret presidential funds, his efforts to recruit support from a dissident wing of the main opposition party fell short, and he found himself impeached and removed from office in December 1993.

A FLAWED SYSTEM?

How to account for this list of failures? Scholars point out that establishing democracy is one thing, while consolidating it is something else entirely. As Dankwart A. Rustow put it, democracy needs time to "habituate" itself.[7] Reformers have stressed the need for time to strengthen state institutions, develop rules and procedures for greater transparency and the rule of law, create and improve political parties and civil society organizations, and build effective working relations between the executive and legislative branches of government. Democratic governments must cope with daunting economic and social challenges and need improved state capacity, accountability, and representativeness in order to meet the stern tests of governance. Donor agencies and international financial institutions have generated long lists of goals, from strengthening local governments to creating more transparent methods for handling legal matters.

Peter Hakim has aptly described the multiple hurdles now facing Latin America's nascent democracies.[8] While he stressed his belief that there is "no single cause or common set of causes that can explain Latin American malaise," he also singled out stronger political parties and better leadership as necessary preconditions for successful governance. From a methodological point of view, it is unclear why the strengthening of particular institutions or sets of institutions should improve the overall rate at which democracies succeed in establishing themselves and remaining functional. Much more work will be needed to enable us to distinguish the truly essential factors from those that are helpful but not crucial.

Studying the failed presidencies may help us make that distinction. Two dynamics are particularly noteworthy. The first flows from the heat that the president and other officials can feel from protest movements seeking concrete solutions to real problems. This is hardly something new in Latin America, where the state—and at its head the president—tends to be seen as the source of all power and the final bearer of responsibility. In many cases, the political costs that came attached to IMF-compliant policies form a prominent theme. Indeed, not only presidents Mahuad and Pérez, but also Argentina's Fernando de la Rúa (driven from office in December 2001) and Bolivia's Gonzalo Sánchez de Lozada (forced out by violent demonstrators in October 2003) felt the sting of protests against austerity measures that each had adopted in order to stabilize a troubled national economy. And yet it is also true that presidents who avoided strong steps for fear of public outcry—this group includes Collor de Mello, Siles Suazo, and Serrano as well as Argentina's Raúl Alfonsín and Ecuador's Abdullah Bucaram—have paid a price for their relative inaction as national currencies collapsed and inflation spiraled out of control.

Protests can present a president with a quandary. Unchecked demonstrations may rage beyond bounds, but the use of force against them can backfire. The personalization of authority in the figure of the president adds a particularly vexing dimension. Failures of government are viewed not as failures of a party or movement, but failures of the chief executive himself. The heavy symbolic trappings carried by the head of state, combined with often-overblown folk memories concerning powerful and nondemocratic past presidents, lead citizens to expect that a leader must fix the country's problems or face bitter charges of incompetence and corruption.

In presidential systems, a crisis will often cease to be primarily about specific grievances and their redress and become instead a question of whether the chief executive himself should go. The police and military, fearing association with an unpopular or discredited leader, may underreact to threats against public order. If unrest mounts, the fixed-term president may find his position growing untenable, with no ready-made exit strategy available to match the dissolution of parliament and call for new elections that would be the solution in a prime-ministerial regime. Pressure from the street (including the worrisome possibility of violence) and congressional actions that push the limits of constitutional propriety may be what it takes to make a failing president face his fate. In the meantime, the political confrontations and turbulence caused by the issue of his removal can threaten to transform a government crisis into a full-blown crisis of the constitutional order itself.

The second dynamic dovetails with the first and helps to explain it. Although the citizenry expects a head of state to resolve deep-seated problems, Latin American democratic presidents are for the most part extraordinarily weak—they "reign" rather than "rule."[9] The weakness of state institutions is usually less at fault than the sheer difficulty of building and maintaining support in a political environment of fragmented parties with little or no internal discipline. Compounding this problem is a lack of institutional incentives to prevent unchecked party splits, floor crossings, and the like. In the absence of majorities in congress, presidents struggle to generate legislative support—only to find that legislators, often of the president's own party, are uninterested in collaborating either with a weak chief executive or contributing to the success of a stronger one. Rather than encourage a logic of cooperation, presidential regimes seem to generate a logic of confrontation precisely because presidential opponents see the success of a president as inimical to their own interests and a failed president as someone to avoid.

The need for a solid capacity to practice the "politics of addition" and build governing coalitions becomes especially apparent when one realizes how many failed Latin presidents have been bereft of *prima facie* majority support. Among the fifteen discussed in this essay, only Haiti's Aristide, Venezuela's Pérez, and Paraguay's Raúl Cubas were elected with absolute majorities. Alfonsín and de la Rúa of Argentina each topped 48 percent, while the remaining ten presidents were runoff winners who came in well short of that in the first round. Fujimori, Serrano, Bucaram, Gutierrez, and Sánchez de Lozada each initially won less than 25 percent of the vote.

At the same time, only Pérez and Cubas (who was Paraguay's chief executive for less than a year in 1998–99) commanded legislative majorities. One study covering all presidential elections in eighteen Latin American countries from 1978 to 2000 found that presidents averaged more than 50 percent of the vote in only half of the countries. Majority legislative support for the president was even rarer, occurring in only about one out of every four presidential terms covered by the study.[10]

The more fragmented the opposition and the smaller the president's own party, the greater becomes the challenge of cobbling together a majority-ruling coalition. Legislators may ignore programmatic considerations entirely and seek instead to gain as many advantages as possible for specific constituency interests. Coalitions will then be short-lived and ad hoc, aimed at grabbing the main chance or weathering the crisis of the moment rather than representing a stable majority of legislators. Even majority coalitions may have little to do with adopting a common program across a range of policy matters. Opposition parties will often stand to get no credit for successful policies but risk blame for failures, giving such parties scant reason to rally to the president, even if promised cabinet posts. Should opposition forces come to think that they might benefit more by causing a president to fail than helping him to succeed, the presidency in question may go into a death spiral. With no prospect of fresh elections to resolve impasses and generate working majorities, executive-legislative relations will wind up bitterly deadlocked in what Juan J. Linz has called the "zero-sum game" of presidentialism.[11]

On the president's side, the travails of coalition building may result from a simple unwillingness to surrender cabinet authority and executive freedom of action to often amorphous and potentially antagonistic partners. Thus for presidents, too, the costs of power sharing may exceed its perceived benefits, leading to the perverse situation of a president who lets his administration remain weak and politically isolated rather than bend his prerogatives to the demands of potential allies.

Although "minority presidents" are more likely to face difficulties than those backed by clear legislative majorities, strong party representation in congress is no guarantee of presidential success. Both Pérez and Cubas disdained dealing with their own parties and faced political revolts (the former's attempt to make up for this by recruiting opposition legislators into a new coalition fell flat, as we have seen). A president may find defeated rivals (perhaps including figures within his own party whom he bested for the nomination) becoming his harshest congressional critics. Aggravating matters, former presidents may be eager to return to office and unafraid to pull their old parties apart in the process.[12] When the going gets rough, allies will desert to save their viability in future elections. In contrast to the situation that obtains in a parliamentary system, legislators can defect without either risking their own seats or affecting the president's ability to remain in office.

To make all this worse, chief executives often find it tempting to attack congress while trying to bypass it with decrees. The precipitous drop in the credibility of legislatures, parties, and politicians—often quite rightly cited as a serious problem in Latin democracies—is due not merely to sensationalist journalism and critical nongovernmental organizations (NGOs) but also to the deliberate rhetoric of presidents who seek to boost their own standing at the legislature's expense. Typically, the more decree powers a president possesses, the worse will be his relations with congress. The exertion of executive prerogatives risks transforming the legislature from an arena for compromise and accommodation into a negative forum aimed at rejecting the executive's agenda. By resorting to decree powers, presidents may become stronger, but the presidential system becomes weaker and more brittle, encouraging confrontation rather than accommodation.

The paradox of Latin American politics is that democratically elected chief executives are undermining democratic institutions in the very act of trying to shore up their own weaknesses as presidents. Even those who do not fail outright all too often leave behind a legacy of missed opportunities. The plebiscitary temptations that come with presidentialism, combined with the popularity of rhetorical assaults on "politics as usual," can lead to an opposite phenomenon: the concentration and even abuse of power in the leader's hands if he succeeds in gaining wide majoritarian support. The cautionary tales of Fujimori, Aristide, and most recently Chávez in Venezuela and Morales in Bolivia show how presidentialism can be perverted into personalistic and quasi-authoritarian rule, although political instability and absence of authority is a far more prevalent pattern.

IS PARLIAMENTARISM THE ANSWER?

These observations suggest that the problem of governance in Latin America may be due to more than just the episodic weaknesses of particular parties, leaders, or institutions. Can it be that presidentialism by its very nature makes confrontations sharper, cooperation more elusive, party discipline harder to achieve, and party fragmentation more likely? Is it time for reformers in the region to think once again about the wisdom of shifting from presidentialism to parliamentary government?[13]

Although "presidentialism" and "parliamentarism" are types that admit of considerable internal variation, and although there are mixed forms of government that combine elements of both, for expository purposes the two systems can be sharply differentiated on several key dimensions.[14] Presidential regimes feature "competing legitimacies." The executive and the legislature can each claim its own electoral mandate to exercise its distinct, though occasionally overlapping powers. Presidents or congresses may choose cooperation or confrontation; the rules of the system (whether formal or informal) fail to require either. Under parliamentary government, by contrast, the legislature generates the executive, which then serves at the pleasure of the legislative majority, whether as a majority or a minority government. Cabinet government means that members of parliament hold responsible executive posts. This not only requires that senior party leaders and would-be ministers must run for legislative office, but also provides a means by which legislators can gain serious executive-branch experience and a more strongly felt stake in how the country's affairs are run, thereby encouraging more skilled and sober leadership.

Under presidentialism, moreover, the chief executive is both head of state and head of government. In the former capacity, the president receives ambassadors and potentates, travels to official funerals, and represents the nation in times of triumph and tragedy. As head of government, the president enjoys wide latitude in naming cabinet and subcabinet officials, although some of these may need legislative consent or be subject to congressional oversight. In parliamentary regimes, the "ceremonial" and "effective" roles are divided, with the head of state (whether a constitutional monarch or a president) filling a symbolic function and perhaps acting as a moderating force at times of crisis. Prime ministers, as executives, run collegial governments that reflect party and coalition imperatives. Although in the media age prime ministers have become more visible as chiefs of government and enjoy considerable authority and prominence in their own right, their post by its very nature still demands that they lead by maintaining the trust of their parties and ultimately a majority of parliament.

Third, the direct election of presidents means that someone may reach the highest office in the land without strong party or governmental experience or support, propelled by direct media appeals in races crowded with candidates. To be successful, a president must work with congress—despite the sometimes overwhelming temptation to bash it—and must achieve this cooperation mostly by using political rather than statutory or constitutional powers. The leadership of the president's own party will be split among congress, the higher levels of the executive branch, and those attached to the party organization. Each of these three groups will often have its own goals and incentives as its members make their various calculations about how best to position themselves for future political success. Prime ministers in cabinet governments are typically not media-driven political amateurs but rather veteran party leaders with substantial ministerial experience and every incentive to stay close to rather than "run against" their own parties and coalition partners in the legislature.

Fourth and finally, presidents and congresses are elected for fixed, often staggered terms, which can lead to a situation where the legislative majority changes hands even while the president has years left in office. In parliamentary regimes, the government can change either when the prime minister's party loses a majority (whether through general-election defeat or a coalition breakup) or when the prime minister's party rebels and calls for new leadership. Any crisis of leadership or government, in other words, trips automatic institutional "safety valves" such as ministerial resignations, parliamentary dissolution, and fresh elections. Crises of government, therefore, rarely become crises of regime. This suppleness of parliamentarism stands in sharp contrast with the intrinsic rigidity of presidentialism, under which a defect in leadership or failure of policy can quickly tailspin into institutional and even mass confrontations with a frightening potential for violent instability and all the human and political costs it portends.

In sum, parliamentary regimes are based on a political logic that encourages cooperation and consensus within the context of coherent policies. The unification of legislative and executive power places a high premium on working together to maximize success and avoid new elections. The underlying logic of presidentialism is far more conflict-prone, meaning that miscalculations or other personal failures of leadership can more easily set loose the perverse logic that leads legislators to hope for the president's failure, particularly late in a term or at a time of special difficulty when citizens become peculiarly eager for a savior—or failing that, a scapegoat.

WHAT'S STOPPING PARLIAMENTARISM?

While the case for adopting parliamentarism might seem compelling to political scientists, the idea of such a shift is plainly anathema to most Latin American citizens. The overwhelming symbolic authority attributed to presidentialism leaps out from the pages of the region's history and bestrides its politics like a colossus. Even if successful democratic presidents have been few and far between, there have been enough legends such as Mexico's Benito Juárez (1861–63, 1867–72) to keep Latin America the continent of presidentialism *par excellence*. Brazil, which is unique in the region for having remained officially a monarchy from the time of its independence in 1822 until 1889, decisively defeated a 1993 referendum on shifting to parliamentarism. The compelling reason seems to have been a fear that doing away with presidentialism would strip citizens of vital representation in the figure of a national leader.

Aside from the potent appeal to tradition, the argument against ditching presidentialism most heard in the region is that parliamentary government would fail precisely because of weak leaders, parties, and legislatures, thereby provoking greater instability. This argument ignores how the political incentive structure based on separation of powers aggravates party fragmentation and indiscipline and encourages weak leadership. It also ignores the substantial evolution in parliamentary governments that has taken place since the wobbliest days of the French Third and Fourth Republics (1870–1940, 1946–58) or the "musical-chairs" cabinets of Italy in the years following World War II.

It is noteworthy that all of the new, post-Soviet democracies of Eastern Europe rejected presidential forms of government, opting instead for semi-presidential systems (based on the French Fifth Republic), where popularly elected presidents with specific powers, including authority in foreign and security matters, coexist with prime ministers whose governments must enjoy the support of parliament to survive.[15] Given Latin Americans' reluctance to abandon the presidential system, semi-presidential formulas might be considered a more realistic alternative. The problem is that semi-presidentialism may not solve some of the inherent problems of presidentialism, and indeed could make them worse by reifying the conflict between the two state powers and personalizing them in the figures of the president and the prime minister.[16]

Preferable to the French-style semi-presidential model would be a parliamentary system with a popularly elected but somewhat less powerful president—something closer to the Portuguese constitutional framework. The power of the president would be specifically limited to a crisis-intervention role when governments need to be formed or parliaments dissolved. The president would not be able to compete with the prime minister in designing or implementing policy. But a parliamentary system with a prime minister beholden to the parliament and a separate elected president would require the adoption of two measures of contemporary parliamentary practice that Portuguese voters have yet to approve: (1) the constructive vote of no confidence, whereby any vote to bring down a government requires proposing a new one; and (2) the option under which the prime minister can declare any legislative proposals a matter of confidence to be approved automatically unless parliament votes to dismiss the government.[17]

TOWARD A LATIN AMERICAN HYBRID? THE FUNDACIÓN MILENIO PROPOSAL

Particularly in the wake of the failure of Brazilians to approve through a national plebiscite a shift away from presidential to parliamentary democracy, it is unlikely that the countries of Latin America will shift away from presidentialism. That does not mean, however, that reforms aimed at achieving greater stability through institutional rules that encourage cooperation and provide safety valves in the face of governmental paralysis are out of the question.[18] Indeed, a recent wave of constitutional engineering in the hemisphere has sought to counteract the negative effects of minority presidencies through such provisions as making elections for president and congress concurrent or by adopting the French "ballotage," which pits the two candidates with the most votes in a runoff election if no candidate succeeds in garnering an absolute majority.

Unfortunately, implementation of the second round may have aggravated the weakness of minority presidencies by encouraging chief executives to believe they had achieved a broad popular mandate and forgetting that they were at best second preferences for a majority of the electorate. More seriously, the "ballotage" tends to dissuade the formation of broad coalitions in support of specific presidential candidacies as parties seek to garner enough support on their own to get into the second round, hoping to win despite the support of a mere plurality of the electorate. This increases the likelihood that the successful runoff candidate will have even less support in the legislature than if he or she had been elected in one round. In Peru, Fujimori surged to 62.5 percent of the vote in the second round after coming in second to Mario Vargas Llosa in the first. And yet, his party garnered only 16.9 percent of the seats in the legislature. Serrano in Guatemala, who would later unsuccessfully try to emulate Fujimori in seeking to shut down the legislature to break the executive-legislative stalemate, obtained 68 percent of the vote in the runoff while securing only 15.5 percent of the seats in the National Congress.

Curiously, recent constitutional reform efforts have not considered an alternative method for generating "majority" presidents: a runoff election in the legislature when no candidate obtains the requisite majority in the electoral college, a variant of the provision in the U.S. Constitution and its Twelfth Amendment. It was the existence of such a provision in the Bolivian Constitution of 1967 that led a broad multiparty commission of Bolivian constitutional scholars and party leaders advised by a team of international experts to propose the adoption of a hybrid system combining essential features of both presidentialism and parliamentarism for consideration by the Bolivian authorities as part of a comprehensive reform of the Bolivian Constitution. The commission was organized by the Fundación Milenio in La Paz and completed its work in 1992. It was led by Juan J. Linz, Sterling Professor of Political Science and Sociology at Yale University.[19]

When the Milenio Commission started its work in Santa Cruz, Bolivia, in 1991, most members favored the adoption of the French "ballottage," arguing that a runoff vote in the legislature that allowed the possible victory of a candidate who did not command the highest plurality of the popular preferences would by definition be less legitimate. And yet commission members soon shifted their views, coming to embrace the notion that in the absence of a clear electoral majority for a particular presidential candidate, the legislature with all of its divergences was intrinsically and more broadly representative of the will of the electorate. This meant that it was perfectly appropriate and legitimate for the legislature to select the candidate that could obtain its endorsement by garnering majority support.

Building on this premise, the Milenio draft constitution made a clear distinction between presidents elected by a majority of the electorate and presidents selected by congressional runoff. The former would derive legitimacy directly from the electorate and would be automatically proclaimed president by the legislature; the latter would derive legitimacy from the legislature. In cases of "grave constitutional crisis and under his exclusive responsibility," presidents elected by electoral majorities would be able to call for the adoption of a vote of confidence by an absolute majority of the members of both legislative chambers. If the president lost the vote, he would be able to call for new elections within ninety days for both the president and the Congress and stand for reelection for another five-year term. At the same time, the legislature could in circumstances of "grave constitutional crisis" remove such presidents by a two-thirds vote of all of its members, a step that would automatically trigger new elections for both the president and Congress within ninety days.

In the alternative scenario, if no presidential candidate received a majority of the popular vote, the Milenio draft prescribes that the candidate with the largest plurality would have five days from the date of the election to obtain congressional ratification as president by proposing to Congress a program of government and the majority coalition that would sustain it. Should he or she fail in that objective, the candidate who achieved the second-highest plurality would have five days to form a government. Should both fail, the Congress would proceed to elect the president by a majority of all of its members through secret ballot, voting as many times as necessary in the case of a tie. The commission included provisions in its draft constitution that would encourage the structuring of governing coalitions based on legislative leadership by permitting members of Congress to take leave to serve as cabinet ministers or diplomats while turning over their legislative duties on a temporary basis to alternates.

In a variation of the constructive vote of no confidence in parliamentary regimes, the president elected through the method of congressional runoff could after one year in office be subject to a motion of censorship, provided it was supported by one-third of all of the members of Congress. Such a motion would lead to the president's removal after seven days if ratified by three-fifths of the members of Congress, and the motion of censure designated a replacement president from Congress's own ranks or from the top three vote getters in the previous presidential race, excluding the censored president. If the motion failed, it could not be presented again for a year. A new president, who would serve out the term of his or her predecessor, would also not be subject to a motion of censorship for at least a year.

The commission clearly eschewed the creation of a dual executive as found in semi-presidential regimes retaining the president as both head of state and head of government. The practical consequences of the proposed reforms, however, would be to introduce a hybrid system of government that would vary depending on the capacity of any given presidential candidate to command the allegiance of a majority of voters. In those cases in which the president was elected by a majority of the electorate, the political system would function more as a classic presidential regime, even if a president did not count on congressional majorities. When presidents were chosen by the legislature in the second round, the political system would function more as a parliamentary form of government, with cabinet officers being drawn from the ranks of Congress and chief executives subject to constructive votes of no confidence. In both cases a resolution to severe institutional deadlock could be sought by calling for new elections. Finally, there was a clear expectation on the part of commission members that given the inability of Bolivian parties to produce strong majorities, Bolivia was more likely to be governed under the second case, accentuating the trend toward a "parliamentarization" of Bolivian politics.

Bolivia's Congress accepted many far-reaching reforms proposed by the Milenio Commission, including reforms of the judicial system, decentralization, and measures to recognize Bolivia's multiethnic society and encourage greater popular participation. However, the reforms described above that would have changed Bolivia's presidential system were not adopted—save a provision that mandated the legislature to select a president from the two, and not three, front-runners in the event that no presidential candidate received an absolute majority of the vote.

Despite Bolivia's checkered history with democratic rule, military withdrawal from politics in the early 1980s led to a surprisingly smooth series of transitions from one elected president to another, including presidents of different parties. In every election, the final outcome had to be determined in the legislature because no president, until Evo Morales in 2005, was able to obtain an absolute majority of the votes. Indeed, on one occasion, the legislature not only did not select the front-runner with the highest plurality of the vote but chose the candidate who had come in third. The choice of the president in the legislature led to a bargaining pattern that encouraged the structuring of multiparty governing coalitions that succeeded at times in carrying out surprisingly far-reaching reforms.[20]

The downside of the politics of compromise in Bolivia was its high degree of fluidity. There was no guarantee that the coalition that initially selected the president in Congress would remain in force, particularly as presidents who gained office with weak mandates lost further ground, finding it increasingly difficult to govern. Without the ability to call for a constructive vote of no confidence or seek an electoral solution to an impasse, presidents resorted to striking deals involving government jobs and patronage. Democracy in Bolivia increasingly projected an image of government as a crass operation to distribute favors among the elite. Parties lost sight of the need to propose programmatic change and continue to revitalize their own institutions and strengthen grassroots support. As a result they discredited themselves with marginalized sectors of society eager for genuine change—a phenomenon that contributed to the rise of Evo Morales and the politics of plebiscitarian populism that is further undermining democratic institutions and norms.

The record of failure displayed by Latin American presidentialism is grave and deeply worrying. It is no exaggeration to say that record is among the reasons why democracy's future now hangs in the balance across a huge swath of the Western Hemisphere. What better moment could there be for citizens throughout Latin America to ask themselves whether their presidentialism traditions are so dear that they must be conserved even at the expense of hopes for democracy's consolidation. The visionary framers who laid down the U.S. Constitution—the model for all pure presidential regimes ever since—had a supreme sense of the peculiarities and even the idiosyncrasies of the particular case for which they were writing a prescription. In their own varying circumstances more than two centuries later, perhaps Latin Americans would do better to imitate the spirit of prudence that actuated the U.S. framers rather than cling to the letter of the system that those framers created. If Latin Americans were to choose such a course, they might also reflect that Europe, in 1787 a haven of autocracy, today can boast models of democratic and predominantly parliamentary governance that experienced significant change and innovation in the post–World War II era and that deserve at least a fair hearing without a priori dismissal merely on the grounds of custom.

APPENDIX

Interrupted Presidencies in Latin America, 1985–2005

Raúl Alfonsín (Argentina, 1983–89). Resigned five months before scheduled transfer of power to newly elected president Carlos Menem with economy spiraling out of control, street demonstrations, and inability to implement policies that were being criticized by successor. Minority president, minority in Congress. No military role. Replaced by elected successor.

Jean-Bertrand Aristide [twice] (Haiti, 1991, 2001–4). Elected in 1990, deposed in 1991 by military coup. Clashes between presidential supporters and opponents. Majority president, minority in Assembly. Replaced by military junta. Elected again in 2000, resigned 2004 amid uprising by former military and deterioration of authority. Authoritarian style of governance, confrontational politics, allegations of corruption. Replaced by Supreme Court chief justice, who is designated provisional president by constitution.

Joaquín Balaguer (Dominican Republic, 1994–96). Reelected to the presidency in 1994 in highly contested election marred by fraud. Massive protests paralyzed country. Agreed to support constitutional changes shortening his term in office by two years. Majority president. No military role. Replaced by elected successor.

Abdalá Bucaram (Ecuador, 1996–97). Elected 1996, resigned six months later in 1997. Economic crisis, allegations of corruption. Minority president, minority in Congress. Military withdrew support after Congress charged him with "mental incapacity." Replaced by congressional appointee as vice president was bypassed.

Fernando Collor de Mello (Brazil, 1990–92). Elected 1989, resigned 1992. Economic crisis, mass demonstrations, allegations of corruption. Minority president, minority in Congress. No military role. Impeached, replaced by vice president.

Raúl Cubas (Paraguay, 1998–99). Elected in 1998, resigned 1999. Resignation triggered by Cuba's pardon of former army commander, sharp splits in ruling party. Assassination of vice president accelerates threat of impeachment amid widespread demonstrations. Congress appoints successor in absence of vice president.

Alberto Fujimori (Peru, 1990–2000). Elected 1990, shut down Congress in 1992 *autogolpe* with strong support of the military. Called for constitutional changes and new election to constitutional assembly. Reelected in 1995 and 2000, resigned in 2000 when majority support in Congress crumbled after contested election and widespread accusations of corruption involving his intelligence chief. Chronic demonstrations against illegal elections and corruption. Military played role in president's decision to leave office. Replaced by congressional appointee; first vice president resigned, second vice president bypassed.

Lucio Gutierrez (Ecuador, 2002–5). Elected 2002, resigned 2005. Gutierrez, a former army officer, had joined junior officers in supporting the demonstrations that let to the resignation of previous president Jamil Mahuad. Elected president with broad support from the Left in 2002, Gutierrez soon ran afoul of his own supporters, who joined with rightist forces in Congress and tried to impeach him. When Gutierrez sought to reorganize the Supreme Court in an attempt to shore up his political support with a new alliance, his actions were widely condemned. Like his predecessor, he faced massive unrest in the streets and was forced to step down when Congress voted to remove him from office.

Jamil Mahuad (Ecuador, 1998–2000). Elected 1988, resigned 2000. Allegations of corruption, mass demonstrations by indigenous groups, splits in ranks of armed forces following protests over IMF-related austerity measures. Minority president, minority in Congress. Military played active role in resignation. Replaced by vice president.

Carlos Andrés Pérez (Venezuela, 1989–93). Elected 1989, resigned 1993. Serious economic crisis, two military coup attempts, allegations of corruption. Majority president, near majority in Congress that crumbled. Impeached. Replaced by congressional appointee.

Fernando de la Rúa (Argentina, 1999–2001). Elected 1999, resigned 2001. Economic crisis, demonstrations and street violence, civilian deaths, allegations of corruption. Minority president, minority in Congress. No military role. Vice president had resigned. Congress appointed a series of successors.

Gonzalo Sánchez de Lozada (Bolivia, 2002–3). Elected 2002, resigned 2003. Mass demonstrations and civilian deaths. Minority president, majority coalition disintegrates. No overt military role. Replaced by vice president.

Jorge Serrano (Guatemala, 1991–93). Elected 1991, resigned 1993 after attempt to close the Congress and arrest members of the Supreme Court. Backdrop of economic crisis leads confrontation with legislature. Minority president, minority in Congress. Military played active role in resignation. Vice president resigned, replaced by congressional appointee.

Hernán Siles Suazo (Bolivia, 1982–85). Elected 1982, agreed to resign one year early in 1985 after Church-brokered agreement. Hyperinflation, failing economic policies, mass demonstrations, civilian deaths, allegations of corruption. Minority president, minority in Congress. Military played active role in resignation. Succeeded by elected president.

CHAPTER SIX

The Predicament of Semi-presidentialism

TIMOTHY J. COLTON AND CINDY SKACH

Following the fall of the Berlin Wall, the hitherto rare constitutional framework known as semi-presidentialism became the modal constitution of the postcommunist world. Combining a popularly elected head of state with a prime minister responsible to the legislature, this framework seemed to many to promise the best of all constitutional worlds. It suggested both the strong leadership of U.S.-style presidentialism and the flexibility of a European-style parliamentary system. Many scholars and practitioners alike considered the combination ideal, and even necessary, for troubled democracies and those countries undergoing democratic transitions.[1]

And yet, the numerous countries that chose semi-presidential constitutions as part of their democratic transitions in the early 1990s have had varied experiences with this constitutional arrangement, as well as with democracy. In many of these countries, the *promise* of semi-presidentialism turned rapidly into the *predicament* of semi-presidentialism, as this constitutional framework began to pose serious design dilemmas and to facilitate democratic backsliding rather than democratic consolidation. Russia is a prime example of this trend.

Russia's long waltz of political transformation has by turns inspired surprise, hope, and disappointment. The initial break with single-party tyranny under Mikhail Gorbachev astonished the Soviet Union—its

Russian core included—and the world. The early days of Boris Yeltsin's presidency generated a wave of optimism that an independent and decommunized Russian state could go on to build an effective democratic polity. The later Yeltsin, however, let down many of those hopes, though not all. Seemingly losing his taste for democratic ways, he took one high-handed step after the other: using force to dissolve an elected parliament in 1993, imposing an unbalanced constitution later that same year, and embarking on a brutal war against secessionists in Chechnya. Under his rule, there was a drift toward aloof and erratic government, characterized by some indigenous observers as "elected monarchy."[2] In 1994, Yeltsin himself referred to Russia as "legalised anarchy."[3]

Yeltsin's handpicked successor, Vladimir Putin, marched much further down that same path after coming to power in 2000. He drew thousands of state security officers into senior positions, oversaw a harsh reoccupation and pacification of Chechnya, curbed media freedoms, recentralized federalism, and took punitive action against members of the budding business elite. Russia's political system today can at best be termed a hybrid of elements of authoritarian rule and liberal residues from the 1980s and 1990s. Some analysts prefer to label it out-and-out authoritarian.[4]

This undemocratic outcome is directly related to the constitutional dynamics in the formative phase of the emerging postcommunist regime. Constitutional development was perhaps more highly contested in Russia than in any of its post-Soviet neighbors. Using Russia as the motivating case, we examine the continuing and emerging problems of an increasingly popular alternative to plain presidentialism or parliamentarism. Does the experience of Russia and the other postcommunist states show that the semi-presidential constitutional framework exacerbates the problems and challenges of democratic governance?

CONSTITUTIONAL TRANSITION

Russia began to debate deep constitutional changes immediately after the semi-competitive election of its new Congress of People's Deputies in 1990, while it was still an integral part of the USSR. Yeltsin, the congress's first chairman, simultaneously chaired a constitutional commission charged with finding a substitute for the Soviet-era basic law. Constitution making was attractive to almost all political players for a variety of reasons: the Soviet federation was crumbling, Russia itself was threatened by internal fissures along territorial and ethnic lines, and a new basis for political legitimacy was needed. Russia's "Brezhnev Constitution," adopted in 1978 (on the heels of the 1977 Soviet Constitution), had been amended several hundred times and was riddled with vague and contradictory clauses. There was a consensus that governmental machinery needed to be revamped in order to effect the promised economic and social reforms, particularly if they were to be resisted by the Soviet authorities.

The constitutional commission came up with a draft by the end of 1990, but further progress was slowed by the increasingly contentious politics of the transition. Yeltsin concentrated on the one adjustment temperamentally most to his liking, and the one that played best to his enormous popularity at the time: the creation of the office of president. Unlike the weak Soviet presidency instituted in March 1990, which Gorbachev was awarded by vote of the Soviet parliament, the Russian president was to be popularly elected. A referendum approved the innovation in March 1991. Yeltsin won the job in a June 1991 landslide, at a time when the economic crisis in Russia was severe: the budget deficit for 1991 was 26 percent of GDP, up from 8.5 percent in 1990.[5] Yeltsin was inaugurated with pomp and circumstance in July. With the failure of the antireform putsch in August and the demise of the Soviet Union that December, he suddenly found himself at the rudder of a sovereign state.

That entity, however, was burdened with a disjointed constitution, which soon was subjected to a fresh round of tinkering and grew increasingly out of sync with reality. When Yeltsin launched his economic "shock therapy" at the beginning of 1992, he largely bowed out of the constitutional debate, ceding the day-to-day leadership of the constitutional committee to its secretary, a young Moscow deputy named Oleg Rumyantsev. In November 1991, the Congress of People's Deputies had given Yeltsin one year to pursue economic reforms. The powers delegated to him to accomplish this included the right to enact special economic reforms by decree, to override previous legislation of the federation, to create or cancel all executive bodies of power, and to suspend any legal acts of local governments which violated the Constitution, or violated the sovereignty of the Russian state, or both.[6] The Supreme Soviet could overrule a presidential decree, but it had to do so within seven days of its original issue.

When that period expired in late 1992, the congress insisted on a larger say in economic policy and pressed for a constitutional solution that would enhance its status. Yeltsin was strongly opposed to this, and the ensuing conflict soon came to a head. After an April 1993 advisory referendum that marginally endorsed his position, followed by the creation of a pro-Kremlin "constitutional assembly" and several months of waffling, Yeltsin in late September peremptorily ordered parliament dissolved and called elections for a new legislature on December 12. When a militant group of deputies resisted, fighting broke out in downtown Moscow, and Yeltsin commanded troops to shell and storm the parliamentary headquarters. Hundreds of lives were lost, and freedoms of assembly and expression were temporarily rescinded. Several weeks later, Yeltsin called for a constitutional plebiscite to be held concurrent with the December 12 parliamentary elections. Although voters returned a parliament full of loosely organized parties largely antagonistic to Yeltsin and his program, they endorsed his proposed Constitution by a comfortable margin. The rules had been tailored to maximize the chances of passage, and some observers even doubt whether the 50 percent requirement was met in reality.[7] It would take a decade and a half until so much as a comma in Yeltsin's Constitution was altered—notwithstanding all of the political and institutional changes, formal and informal, that took place over that time.

CONSOLIDATING A FLAWED SYSTEM

In the semi-presidential constitutional arrangement, also known as a dual-executive system, a popularly elected head of state coexists with and shares executive power with a prime minister (chairman of the Council of Ministers) who is nominated by the president but confirmed by and responsible to the legislature. The simultaneous existence of two executives is the outstanding and unique feature of semi-presidentialism. Such power sharing by definition excludes a neat division of authority and leads to constitutional ambiguity. The legitimacy, accountability, and responsibility of

TABLE 6.1
The Balance of Power in Semi-presidential Systems

Consolidated Majority	Divided Majority	Divided Minority
President and prime minister have same majority in legislature	Prime minister has majority, president does not	Neither president nor prime minister has majority
Presidential hegemony	Cohabitation	Power vacuum

these two executives are fundamentally different: the prime minister emanates from the legislature and must answer to it, whereas the president has much greater autonomy from the legislature and can survive without its approval. This autonomy allows the president to push his own agenda, even if it means invading the prime minister's domain. Tensions between the president, the prime minister, and the legislature are inherent in the structure of semi-presidentialism and are therefore permanent. But the presence of a legislative majority, and a mutually supportive relationship between that majority and both executives, can minimize the probability that these tensions result in serious institutional conflict.

In terms of the balance of authority and power within the institutional realm, we distinguish three different possibilities, each of them rooted in electoral rules and realities (see Table 6.1).[8] In the first and least conflictual possibility, the popularly elected president is a party man, and both he and the prime minister are supported by the same legislative majority. This produces what may be called *consolidated majority government.* In a second and more problematic outcome, the president does not have a legislative majority, but the prime minister does. This is a *divided majority government*, or what is commonly referred to as *cohabitation*. In the third and most conflict-ridden semi-presidential outcome, neither the president nor the prime minister has a legislative majority. This is a *divided minority government.*

In practice, divided minority government combines the most problematic kind of presidential government (divided government) with the most problematic kind of parliamentary government (minority government). The president is divided from the legislature, and at the same time the legislature is divided against itself. Adding insult to injury, the president is usually also divided against the prime minister. It is in this most difficult subtype of the semi-presidential model that Russia spent the formative part of its postcommunist lifespan.

Divided minority government is particularly vulnerable to democratic breakdown. The absence of any clear majority leads to an unstable scenario, characterized by shifting legislative coalitions and government reshuffles on the one hand, and continuous presidential intervention and use of reserved powers on the other hand. The greater the legislative immobilism, governmental instability, and cabinet reshuffling that result from failed majorities, the more institutional incentives presidents have to dominate the political process and rule by decree.

The worst problems start here, because divided minority government can be a slippery slope to dictatorship. A president who relies extensively on decrees and ignores the democratically elected legislature may move the country toward constitutional dictatorship, narrowing the decision-making arena to a small number of handpicked nonparty technocrats.[9] This technocratization of the cabinet hinders the democratic principles of inclusion and contestation, distances the government even further from the legislature, and cramps parliamentary responsibility. Divided minority government is most likely to arise in the context of an inchoate and fragmented party system, in which there are no party coalitions and the president considers himself to be "above" the political parties.

Most people associate the semi-presidential constitution with the French Fifth Republic (1958–). France has had an atypical and very fortunate experience with semi-presidentialism, however. For two decades after the first direct presidential election in 1965, it enjoyed consolidated presidential and legislative majorities in the National Assembly, and so avoided the more conflictual subtypes of the model. Even a short period of divided minority government from 1988 to 1993 did not threaten French democracy, because by that time the country's party system was well structured and the president, François Mitterrand, was a party man well integrated into that system. As a result, even during these rare minority years France managed to stay off the slippery slope toward constitutional dictatorship.

RUSSIA'S UNFORTUNATE BEGINNINGS

Russia was a very different story. From its inception, Russian semi-presidentialism was of the most conflict-ridden subtype—divided minority government—and so it remained for the rest of the country's first post-communist decade. Importantly, unlike his counterparts in Paris, President Yeltsin never enjoyed a consolidated presidential and legislative majority. When in 1998–99 the Left-leaning prime minister Yevgenii Primakov got close to mustering a working majority in the Duma, Yeltsin, as the other half of this dual executive, sacked Primakov prematurely. These presidential–prime ministerial dynamics, structured by the Constitution, worked against democracy by sending negative messages to those willing and able to build sustainable party majorities.

The deep roots of Russia's constitutional imbroglio lay in the politics of the late-Soviet and early post-Soviet periods. In the mature Soviet system, formal constitutional provisions were a polite cover for the control exercised by the Communist Party. The USSR's "dignified" Constitution—Walter Bagehot's famous term for the document's symbolic part[10]—laid out a two-chamber parliament (the Supreme Soviet); a prime minister and government responsible to it; and, as an executive capstone, a collective Presidium of the Supreme Soviet, which from the late 1970s was chaired by the general secretary of the Communist Party. Everyone knew that according to the country's "efficient" Constitution—Bagehot's term for the way things actually work and get done—the Party's leader and the Politburo called the shots.

The situation became unstable with the onset of political liberalization in the late 1980s. Yeltsin became chairman of the Russian legislative branch and subsequently hopped to the newly created Russian presidency, somewhat mimicking Gorbachev's jump from Communist Party secretary to president of the USSR in 1990—with the difference that Yeltsin was directly elected by the population. The creation of Yeltsin's new post endowed Russia with the essentials of a semi-presidential system. Put in place by the nation, the president had the highest symbolic standing, but the Congress of People's Deputies and the Supreme Soviet remained intact. So did a separate governmental cabinet and prime minister, nominated by the president but confirmed by the Supreme Soviet as well as the archaic Presidium.

Until 1993 the biggest threat to the Russian president's authority was not the prime minister, however, but the chairman of the multi-tiered parliament. During his brief tenure in that post in 1990, Yeltsin had accumulated fairly extensive powers: control over the legislative agenda; filtration of proposed appointments to ministerial and other positions; issuance of binding decrees through the Presidium; and reporting to congress on all matters concerning the state of the federation, foreign and domestic affairs, and national security. His successor as chairman, a one-time loyalist of his, Ruslan Khasbulatov, inherited most of those powers and did his best to augment them. Thus, although the president had his sheaf of prerogatives, many of his powers overlapped with those of the Supreme Soviet chairman.

Given the highly fluid, poorly institutionalized party system, neither executive could count on a solid party majority in the legislature. As a result, Russia found itself with a divided minority government from day one. It was a highly unstable structure, because neither executive had a legislative majority, but both had substantial access to decree-making authority for bypassing the other branches of government. In short, "the stage was set for collision."[11]

The clash was not long in coming, encouraged by the institutional duality of the semi-presidential framework. Both the president and the Supreme Soviet chairman treated the government apparatus as beholden to them, issuing direct orders to officials and agencies at all levels. Both were entitled to initiate legislative proposals. The president had a limited veto over bills passed by parliament, but no right to dissolve parliament and force new elections. Depriving him of that right while giving him the power to declare a state of emergency and putting him in charge of the armed forces and the Security Council denied him recourse to normal democratic exits from conflictual situations while bestowing upon him the weapons to impose his own solutions.

The congress and the Supreme Soviet, for their part, could force a government's resignation through a no-confidence vote or by obstruction of presidential initiatives—as happened in December 1992 with the "government of young reformers" headed by Yegor Gaidar, who was replaced by

Viktor Chernomyrdin, a veteran of the Soviet industrial bureaucracy. The tools for determining exit and resolving government crises before they ripened into regime crises were awarded principally to the legislature, not to the president. Consequently, the president had a greater incentive to escalate conflict against other government institutions to an extraordinary level, so as to capitalize on his unique resources. An unsatisfactory constitutional formula was introduced and consolidated, initiating a path dependence that was difficult to escape.[12]

This is not to say that constitutional clashes were the only ones that mattered—far from it.[13] Conflicts raged over numerous other questions, principally those surrounding market reforms and the distribution of property; on most matters, the parliament tended to take a more conservative tack, while Yeltsin's executive team took a more radically reformist stance. While not necessarily overshadowing these other conflicts, constitutional issues resonated with them and made their resolution incomparably more difficult. In short, the semi-presidential Constitution polarized the field of political action rather than facilitated the resolution of disagreements. Legislators such as Khasbulatov and Rumyantsev slid from moderate to belligerently anti-presidential positions on economic and social issues, partly so as to attract support from those who favored a more balanced constitution. The president's camp increasingly avoided bargaining with the legislators, concentrating on dispensing patronage to the more liberal of them and writing off the rest as hopelessly reactionary and power mad.

TOWARD CONSTITUTIONAL DICTATORSHIP

Some of the political problems Russia had suffered since 1990 bedeviled the constitutional settlement dictated by Yeltsin in December 1993. While technically semi-presidential, Yeltsin's Constitution gave the president notoriously strong and often unilateral power. Article 90(1), for example, stipulates that "the president of the Russian Federation issues decrees and directives," the only restriction being that these cannot contradict existing laws. If we measure the de jure powers of the presidents in Russia, the French Fifth Republic, and Weimar Germany, the Russian president is constitutionally almost twice as powerful as the president of the Fifth

Republic, and at least one-third more powerful than was the president of the Weimar Republic.[14]

Before and especially after Vladimir Putin's presidential accession in 2000, critics in Russia and elsewhere have often labeled the Russian system "super-presidential" and have linked it directly or indirectly to the country's antidemocratic trend.[15] Under Yeltsin, the tilting of the balance toward the presidency was not enough to produce effortless domination, and he in any case was willing to settle for cooperation from the legislature and not total control. After the adoption of the 1993 Constitution, the president and parliament continued to derive separate legitimacy from their modes of election, pursued different priorities, and jockeyed for momentary advantage. The 1995 parliamentary election returned a corps of deputies more splintered and more antipathetic to the president than the 1993 parliament, and Yeltsin's reelection in 1996 subsequently opened a new round of hostilities.

Legislative immobilism and governmental instability gave Yeltsin abundant incentives to strike out on his own and rule by executive decree. Although he did have greater recourse to legislation in the late 1990s, his lack of a stable legislative majority combined with his extensive presidential powers made him resort to unilateral directives at moments of peril. Parliament retaliated in kind by subjecting the president to a lengthy impeachment ordeal in the wake of the August 1998 financial crisis. The indictment, dredging up all manner of grievances from the previous decade, narrowly failed to pass in May 1999.

Since 1993, Russia's governance has continued to suffer from some of the same infirmities that beset it in the period of outright breakdown. More corrosive of democracy, the institutionalized disagreement rampant in 1990–93 was used to justify authoritarian tendencies put forward in the name of political normalization and social progress. This allowed Yeltsin in the 1993 Constitution to get rid of the legislative Presidium and the strong parliamentary chairmanship, thereby appropriating many of the powers that had eluded him before: the power to dissolve the lower house (the State Duma) for cause; a monopoly over all ministerial appointments other than that of the prime minister; the nearly unrestricted right to emit decrees; and the effective immunity of the presidential establishment and the bureaucracy from legislative oversight. Several presidential powers could only be checked by the Federation Council rather than by the State Duma.[16] Again, all of this was Yeltsin's preference. Realizing the need for majority support and noting his lack of such support in the State Duma, Yeltsin arranged for this prerogative to be given to the Federation Council. At the time, very few representatives of political parties or movements sat in the council; instead, it was dominated by nonpartisan regional elites who generally favored Yeltsin's politics because they had been appointed by him or, if elected, enjoyed his support and patronage.[17]

To be sure, Yeltsin refrained from using these vast powers to destroy his opposition, squelch free speech, or abrogate competitive elections. In fact, he studiously refused to insert himself into the arena of mass politics except during presidential election campaigns; he also rejected repeated suggestions that he form a pro-presidential and pro-reform political party. As a side effect, his lack of a party base may have left him vulnerable to covert influence by "the oligarchs" (Russia's new business moguls) and sundry wheeler-dealers.

Putin possesses few of Yeltsin's inhibitions against the unbridled use of executive power. He encouraged the creation of the pro-Kremlin party United Russia, which in December 2003 along with its coalition partners gained two-thirds of the State Duma's 450 seats. He used "administrative levers" and the freedom of the president from parliamentary and popular scrutiny to reverse many of the democratizing political innovations instituted under Yeltsin and, for that matter, under Gorbachev. More even than Yeltsin, he saw and sees government as a closed preserve to be managed by nonparty technocrats, bureaucrats, and insiders unconnected to the realm of party and mass politics. This disassociation of cabinets and governmental policy making from the legislature hinders the democratic principles of inclusion and contestation and terribly cramps parliamentary responsibility.

It was one thing for Yeltsin to rationalize Kremlin-centered government as an antidote to extreme political fragmentation and a battering ram to push through long-delayed modernizing reforms. It was another thing for Putin—appropriating and extending the institutional legacy left by his less autocratic predecessor—to exalt executive dominance within a "strong state" as a formula of indefinite duration. With his personal popularity riding high, government ministers serving at his whim, a disciplined parliament, the autonomy of the regional governors circumscribed, the business magnates cowed by arrests of several of their number, a subservient national television, and the policy process almost totally closed, Putin governed with few effective checks and balances. It is not coincidental that in 2005, Freedom House, for the first time since Soviet days, classified Russia as a "Not Free" political system, lumping it with countries like Turkmenistan, Uzbekistan, and Belarus. By and large, Yeltsin's liberal market reforms remained in force and continued to help the Russian economy expand, although even here the state presence in export-oriented industries increased, and anticorruption laws were used selectively against political enemies, as demonstrated by the attack on oil magnate Mikhail Khodorkovsky. In the political domain, though, most movement was backward.

CONSTITUTIONAL ALTERNATIVES

Might post-Soviet Russia have turned out otherwise? Playing with historical counterfactuals is a fascinating but slippery intellectual game. And yet, things surely could have taken a somewhat different trajectory if key players had ranked the achievement of constitutional equilibrium and political openness high on their list of objectives. The curious institutional legacy of Soviet rule and early post-Soviet changes would not have been easy to overcome, but nothing suggests it would have been impossible.

The personalization of power in Russia went to such extremes that we must acknowledge that, unlike in 1990 or 1993, some key outcomes hinged on the preferences of a single man. Had Putin wished it so—like Charles de Gaulle in France's Fifth Republic—he undoubtedly could have brought about a more transparent and polycentric institutional order in Russia. It is true that de Gaulle had a more structured party system to work with than Putin, but the examples of Gorbachev and Yeltsin show that leaders in closed systems can indeed learn from experience and change their minds, even when the party context is not particularly supportive of change. Such is the value of innovative, forward-looking leadership. Nothing about Putin's record, however, indicates that he ever wished to endow Russia's political system with greater inclusion and contestation—the two crucial dimensions of democracy.[18]

Putin as president repeatedly said that he did not favor constitutional change, seeming to view it as a Pandora's Box best left unopened. This resistance broke down, and a number of other political variables changed, when his second term as president ended in 2008. Putin did not attempt to amend the Constitution to allow him to serve as president for more than the mandated two consecutive terms. He put forward a protégé, Dmitrii Medvedev, as his favored candidate for president, and Medvedev easily won election in March 2008. In May Medvedev was sworn in and Putin went off, not into retirement but to the *other* half of Russia's dual executive: the prime ministership. From this position, he is far more involved in peak decisions than any of his or Yeltsin's prime ministers were, and Medvedev gives every appearance so far of being a weak chief executive, perhaps a mere figurehead. In November 2008 Medvedev announced that the government would push through a constitutional amendment extending the president's term in future from four years to six years. Having stepped out of the presidency for a time, Putin has every chance to return to the position, should he so desire, and this time to serve for two six-year terms. Depending on when such a change occurred, he could rule unchallenged until his seventieth birthday in 2022 or even later.[19]

Unlike Yeltsin, Putin became a "majority man" when it came to relations with parliament. In 2004, he proposed an alteration of the electoral law that would require all Duma deputies to be elected on a party-list system, subject to a 7 percent electoral threshold. The change, approved in 2005, went into effect in the 2007 parliamentary elections, in which United Russia won 315 of the 450 Duma seats. Putin, while still president, stood at the head of the United Russia candidates' list in December 2007; in April 2008, shortly before becoming prime minister, he took over leadership of United Russia. All indications are that he may use this position to move further in an authoritarian direction and to limit the "sites of competition" that are normally open to both government and opposition in a healthy democracy.

BEYOND THE PREDICAMENT

The Russian case sadly, but clearly, shows that if a democratizing country is not able to build genuine legislative majorities and ensure that presidents are integrated into an institutionalized party system, it will most likely operate under the semi-presidential arrangement that we refer to as divided minority government. It was during the intense crisis period of divided minority government in 1993 that Yeltsin took Russia largely out of the democratic box and pushed through a constitution that boosted the power of the presidency.

Most new democracies have poorly institutionalized party systems, such as Russia's has been, and presidents who present themselves, at least initially, as being "above" the political parties. Semi-presidentialism tends to lock in conflictual patterns of executive-legislative behavior. For example, nearly all the former Soviet republics except for the three Baltic states chose semi-presidentialism at independence, and virtually all of them have suffered crises involving their dual executives. Some have moved away from the model, only to drift back. In Ukraine, for example, constitutional amendments trimming the president's powers and strengthening the legislature accompanied the "Orange Revolution" of late 2004. But in 2006 the new president, Viktor Yushchenko, proposed a change in the opposite direction, to be ratified by a constitutional referendum. These developments stand in stark contrast to other semi-presidential countries in Europe, such as Poland and Portugal, where key executives chose to push their constitutions toward a more parliamentary model by decreasing presidential powers and strengthening such institutions as the constitutional courts.

So what does the postcommunist experience tell us about the democratic performance of semi-presidentialism? In 2004, eight postcommunist countries of east-central Europe were admitted to the European Union. Their membership was contingent on the fulfillment of the political criteria laid down at the European Council's 1993 Copenhagen summit.[20] Of these eight, five were parliamentary (Hungary, Czech Republic, Slovakia, Estonia, and Latvia), and three were semi-presidential (Poland, Lithuania, and Slovenia). The three semi-presidential countries all have in common that their leadership and governing styles have become more party-oriented over time. Political leaders *and* parties have been crucial to this evolution. By becoming more party-oriented, leaders were able to nudge their countries closer to the purely parliamentary constitutional model, over time decreasing the power of the presidency and balancing the presidency with other institutions.

Poland is an interesting case of semi-presidentialism and democratic evolution in this regard. In 1997, the president and prime minister, supported by a legislative majority, reduced presidential power and increased the power of the Constitutional Tribunal. President Aleksander Kwaśniewski was asked why these reforms were not adopted earlier in the country's democratic transition, which could have saved Poland from its early years of destabilizing institutional conflict. He replied that, although it was clear that Poland should move in the direction of a parliamentary system, such a move was only possible once there was a majority of political parties that together controlled both the presidential and legislative branches.[21]

Both the quality and the shape of parties and party systems are critical for enhancing the performance of semi-presidentialism and for overcoming the semi-presidential predicament. Unfortunately, parliamentary majorities, and presidents who are supported by and supportive of these majorities, remain rare in new democracies. All this indicates that a country's best chance for reducing conflict in the context of semi-presidentialism may be to follow the Portuguese and Polish examples and limit the powers of the president—especially emergency and decree powers and control over the military. As presidential powers are reduced, and if other institutions such as constitutional courts are strengthened, the result is a constitutional arrangement that looks rather more like parliamentarism; we might tentatively dub it "parliamentarizing semi-presidentialism." And as the evidence from the new EU members indicates, there is a good chance that the end result of this parliamentarization will be more democracy.

Even the French, who have lived with semi-presidentialism for over forty years, questioned and reformed their Constitution in 2002. As noted above, France's experience with semi-presidentialism has been more fortunate than that of the post-Soviet states. The French enjoyed consolidated presidential and legislative majorities in the National Assembly for two continuous decades after the first direct presidential election in 1965. Eventually, however, tensions in the model also emerged in France, as majorities began to break down and periods of cohabitation became more frequent. Politicians, as well as three-fourths of the public, blamed elements of semi-presidentialism for France's institutional conflict. The Socialist Party made a referendum on institutional reform a central part of its 2007 presidential-campaign platform.[22]

In its French incarnation, semi-presidentialism led to a situation in which Gaullist president Jacques Chirac locked horns with Socialist prime minister Lionel Jospin and his *majorité plurielle*. In September 2002, the French voted in favor of reducing the presidential mandate from seven to five years, hoping to eliminate the often turbulent periods of cohabitation and dual-executive crisis altogether. And France, it goes without saying, is a consolidated democracy.

It is time for Russia, along with the many other fragile democracies that suffer from the semi-presidential predicament, to rethink its constitutional framework. Constitutional and de facto changes in France, but also in Poland and Portugal, further inspire our conclusions. We believe this is an opportune moment for leaders to use these important examples of double institutional evolution (that is, more parliamentarism and more democracy) to reconfigure constitutionalism in the twenty-first century, in Russia and elsewhere.

Conclusion

The Way Forward

FERNANDO HENRIQUE CARDOSO

It is striking that hardly three decades after the Third Wave of democratization, a book is already being published with the title *Democracies in Danger.* What are these risks? Elective incompatibilities—reversing Goethe's expression—between the "Third Wave" societies and the democratic political institutions? Incapacity of democratically elected governments to satisfy the needs and aspirations of their population? Cultural impossibilities that restrict the practices of representative democracy to the countries of the "West"? But aren't Latin American countries, in their vast majority, culturally and geographically part of what we might call the "Far West"? And, conversely, haven't some countries of the East and of Central Europe been able to reshape democratic values and embed them in everyday politics (consider Japan or even Poland or some Baltic countries from the former Soviet sphere)?

This book, from the comprehensive introduction by Alfred Stepan to the penetrating analysis of specific situations, significantly helps us to reframe the questions of democracy in the contemporary world in the light of new realities, both at the societal and at the institutional level. Suffice it to mention as an example the excellent synthesis of the conflictive relations evolving within civil society made by Ashutosh Varshney, highlighting the complexity of the racial, territorial, religious, and political dimensions that characterize the ethnic interactions in local communities. Or the no-less-insightful chapter by Timothy Colton and Cindy Skach about the Russian type of semi-presidentialism.

It is not necessary to review in this conclusion each chapter's contribution to bring forth the new: Stepan has done that in his introduction. I will limit myself to a few points, actually two, that may add or give more emphasis to the book's content. And I will confine myself to discussing the situations that I am more familiar with, those of South America, to extract from the recent developments in the region a reflection about the resilience of corporativism and patrimonialism and about the absence of the "democratic spirit." Let us start by this last point.

It is well known that in the discussion of the founding fathers of the American democracy, the scaffolding was deemed less important than the inspiring ideals of the democratic construction. Faithful to old Greece, they loathed tyranny and strove to strengthen the values that would prevent the domination of a few over the many. The sole sovereign was the people. And often they evoked a formula hardly used today: the pursuit of people's happiness. The emphasis on this theme in Thomas Jefferson's letters is quite remarkable. But Jefferson was not the only one to mention the idea. Nor did he and the other theorists (and practitioners) of the American democracy restrict themselves to this issue.

Confronted with the English tradition (fearful of a possible return to monarchy) and the passion for the French Revolution, the founding fathers paved the way for the strengthening of the *res publica* in an apparently straightforward way, but almost invariably embedded their knowledge of the classics. Reading through the Federalist Papers proves this point all too well. They fled, as the devil from the cross, from "democracy" in its original Greek sense—the *agora* with the presence of citizens and, later, its demagogic degeneration with the advent of the mob. They realized that the general will, in a complex society, could not be reduced to this form of manifestation. They thus loved representation as the legitimate foundation of the popular will.

The founders of the American democracy did not put their trust on Montesquieu's "spirit of the laws" as justification for adopting a relativistic view concerning the forms of government that would be influenced by geographical and social determinants. To organize the Republic, however, they did not despise the separation and balance of powers. They put their emphasis not so much on "freedom" in the French sense but on the freedoms guaranteed by institutions. Moreover, they envisioned the laws, with a jusnaturalist foundation, as the process through which the legislative bodies distilled what customary behavior had naturally molded. They believed that the freedom of the individual was the moral foundation of associative life. Living in community was not an external imposition but rather a need felt by the citizenry that, for this very reason, accepted the limitations to each one's freedom to preserve everyone's freedom. Law was, therefore, the condition of conviviality. And equality under the law stemmed from the conviction that all men are born equally fit to freedom, which is the natural right of each and every one.

Within this framework, in which the acknowledged sovereignty lay with the people, and in which law was at the same time the foundation of each person's freedom and the safeguard of everyone's, the judiciary gained special relevance—even more so considering that a large portion of its officials would be directly selected through elections as an expression of the popular will. The judge, in this sense, was considered to be the guarantor and the interpreter of the rules of conviviality and of respect to the private sphere. The Supreme Court, interpreter of a non-casuistic Constitution, safeguarded the rules of the democratic interplay and the "spirit of freedom" against any usurper, be it the legislative or the executive branch.

Behind these constructions lay what Tocqueville had keenly grasped: a certain condition of equality, deriving from the coexistence between the "spirit of religion" and the "spirit of freedom" as well as from the widespread right to own land prevailing in New England. Thomas Jefferson, using surprisingly modern words, proclaimed it a principle that set limits to the right of individual property. Religion, according to Tocqueville, saw in civil freedom the noble exercise of human faculties, and in the political domain the terrain left open by the Creator to the work of intelligence. From the compatibility between these two "spirits," of freedom and of religion, as experienced in the New Colony, resulted that "freedom sees in religion . . . the divine source for its own rights. It considers religion as the safeguard of custom; customs as the insurance of the laws and pledge of their own durability" (*Democracy in America*, 197).

It is not hard to argue that the foundations of power in Latin America stem from other sources. Even disregarding the weight of the Iberian tradition, with its patrimonialism and even autocratic personalism, and moving away from "culturalistic" interpretations, it is enough to read Arturo Valenzuela's chapter on Latin America's interrupted presidencies to understand the differences between the United States and the Latin American situations. The personalization of authority in the figure of the president and the party fragmentation arising from the disconnection between the voter's will and the representative's behavior are manifest signs of the lack of belief in the "spirit of freedom" grounded on the citizens' natural rights.

Our political systems bear the stamp of a paradox: a huge expectation is invested in the head of state, the holder of authority, but this is contradicted by a democratic institutional architecture based on factions and particular interests alien to the logic of submission to the head of state. Elections to the presidency and to congress tend to differ in the way they generate and reflect prevailing political preferences and interests in society, even though they take place at the same time. The former tends to produce a majority will invested in the head of state, which is seldom replicated in the distribution of seats in congress. Thus, only in some rare occasions does the president find, from the start, a solid majority in the legislative branch, enabling them to fulfill the expectations of the population. Hence the conflicting character of the relation between the legislative and executive branches that typifies Latin American presidentialism. The political system is ruled by the logic of confrontation, far from the logic of cooperation, of harmony between the branches of power, foreseen by Montesquieu.

The outcome of these inconsistencies has been outlined by Valenzuela: interrupted presidencies, political and administrative failures, incapacity of presidents and government to deliver. And yet, oddly, some insist on defining Latin American presidential style as "imperial." In fact, the "imperial" dimension of the presidents of the countries in the region that follow democratic rules is more appearance than reality. The recent strengthening of the institutions, especially of congresses, pushes presidents to ground their governments on ad hoc coalitions, dependent on the nature of the issues at hand. The executive branch often lacks political support to implement its plan of government, insofar as there are no political parties in the strong sense of the term or, when they exist, they seldom form a majority in congress, since the mechanics of electoral systems rarely allow such result. Even when presidentialism proves to be relatively successful, as in Brazil, parliamentary support is obtained at great cost. The interplay between executive and legislative branches bears the price of popular disenchantment toward political parties and congresses, and ultimately towards the presidents themselves.

It is true that Chile and Uruguay are exceptions where the strength of political parties is effective, as they are deeply rooted on national political life, while in others countries, like Mexico, in spite of the existence of traditional and strong parties, recent democracy has not yet managed to harmonize the relations between the branches of power. This situation has been at the root of repeated deadlocks.

From a historical point of view, the impression one has is that in Latin America the democratic form—and I underline the word *form*—seems to function without internal frictions only in more traditional situations (Uruguay or even Colombia, despite the guerrillas), in which the historical power holders have not yet been strongly challenged by the rise of a mass society. When such a society emerges, as in Mexico or Argentina, without the appropriate strengthening of the "democratic spirit" or, in better words, without a democratic culture embedded in society, then either the president indeed becomes "imperial," or the situation leads to an institutional deadlock.

A certain condition of equality, a component highlighted by Tocqueville as a homogenizing factor in American politics, withers away in Latin America under the historical burden of property concentration and, until today, of income concentration. In socioeconomically fractured societies, political representation, if we can speak of representation at all, is also diffused and fragmented. It lacks political and cultural conditions to assure substance to the popular delegation and hence legitimacy to congressional decisions as well as congruence between the aspirations leading to the presidents' elections and the behaviors of legislators. Commitments with a broader political scope are tenuous. The representatives have plenty of space for the negotiation of specific interests, and also to serve well-defined purposes, thus establishing a linkage between congress and the social fabric. It could even be said that congress tends to become the clearinghouse for lobbies and corporative connections. But congress is missing the flame of dedication to the general interest needed to give the country the sense that, in democracy, government, parliament, and society find appropriate and compatible institutional spaces to pursue consensual objectives, if not purposes expressing the will of the majority, while respecting the viewpoints of the minority. The minority, in any case, keeps the perspective of a power shift in the incoming elections.

Despite the fragility of linkages between the behavior of parliament members and the sentiment of the electorate with respect to their interests, congressional institutions, at least in some countries, are solid and well geared. In these, the architecture of democracy, its scaffolding, is visible and functions smoothly. Elections are regularly held, laws are produced. Executive branch decisions and decrees are often criticized, and so on and so forth. The interests and even some values of segments of the society are reflected on the legislative institutions. But they do not necessarily coalesce around consistent political philosophies or viewpoints that would allow an informed choice about the general objectives to be pursued.

Often the connection between legislators and some social segments is established after the election, not as an outcome of policy stands taken during the electoral campaign. In this way, the political parties, through some of their members, "reflect"—more than represent—interests that are fragmentarily scattered all over society and are prismatically mirrored in the legislative branch. These interests are not connected to values; they do not arise out of a proposal or philosophy capable of, using a classic expression, bringing happiness to people. The machinery of democratic institutions grinds forward, but it lacks the soul, the "spirit," that should nurture it: the belief in the formal equality under the law, applicable to all, the search for the general interest and a pathway to greater social equality.

The saying that comes from the nineteenth century is still valid: to the enemies, the law; to friends, everything, starting with the approval of the measures that benefit them. In these conditions, the persistence of coups against constitutions and the overthrow of presidents are hardly amazing. Yesterday, coups d'état were militarily imposed. Today they enjoy popular support. Love of freedom is relative, and the incompetence of governments, or their inability to satisfy society's expectations, heightened by democratization itself, paves the way for the emergence of demagogues, of "saviors" of the nation. The citizenry, if we can use this word to qualify the electoral masses, does not feel engaged in and concerned with the decisions taken by the democratic state in the conditions under which it operates. The consequence is the emergence of what has been criticized in Brazil since the imperial period: a gap between "public opinion," namely, the informed opinion, and "national opinion," namely, the perception of the majority of the population. The latter is less connected with everyday politics but no less aware of their immediate interests, and no less politically important, as they account for the majority of voters.

In this interplay between an executive from which one expects everything and that cannot meet those expectations, and a congress that is a patchwork of specific interests without a philosophy linking the legislators' will to that of their respective parties, the balance between powers is fragile. This is made even more difficult by the fact that the judiciary in Latin American lands, with the exception of a few countries such as Brazil, lacks the authority and sometimes even the autonomy or means to enforce the letter and, to a greater extent, the "spirit" of the constitution, which, incidentally, is often ambiguous.

It is understandable that, confronted with such a picture, one continues to search for institutional solutions for the region's political crisis. The script and the actors may change: yesterday generals were responsible for the crisis, today this role is played by plebiscitary *caudillos*. Yesterday, dictatorships followed an unacceptable script; today it is generalized corruption or governments' inefficiency to satisfy people's demands. We thought, until recently, that the parliamentary system might be able to strengthen the parties and lead to institutional forms that would enhance collaboration rather than conflict among branches of power. Today, as pointed out by Arturo Valenzuela, there is an exploration by political leaders and scholars of the possibilities of the French or Portuguese model of semi-presidentialism. There may be some sense of progress in these formulas, always with the caveat that the analysis of what is happening in Russia or even in France requires.

As a matter of fact, there is criticism about the way semi-presidentialism works even in some mature democracies. In a book published in

2007, *L'Impasse,* Lionel Jospin, criticizing the French Fifth Republic with the authority of a former prime minister, did not hesitate to indicate pure presidentialism as his preferred choice.[1] The ambiguities between a president supposed to be apart and above government and the prime minister, based on a parliamentary majority, give rise to conflicts that can hardly be managed in a way consistent with the general interest. In this sense, inclination toward a strong leader would not only be an expression of the "Russian soul," where the president is seen as a czar; the search for a more clearly defined and stronger center of power, according to Jospin's analysis, would also stem from the very nature of the semi-presidential system that gives birth to gray zones with ambiguous power competencies.

There are several possible institutional solutions to minimize the crises undermining the functioning of the democratic system. To deal with the Latin American difficulties, I would not rule out even the return to a reflection about parliamentarism, provided it is an authentic one: with single-member district systems, reduction in the number of parties, creative forms to expand the electorate's participation in the decision-making process, and so on. However, I do think that without a strong advocacy for democracy that emphasizes and enforces the principle of the rule of law without "a certain condition of equality" (in particular, that of opportunities, which implies an educational revolution and broader economic access), the fragmentation of societies, the excluded masses, and the clash of interests among the power elites will hardly lead to greater political stability in some countries of the region. We are lacking a strong faith in democracy itself. Without democrats, how can democratic institutions be sustained?

I do not say this to add to today's prevailing pessimism. Contrary to that pessimism, I do think that, while there are grounds for a gloomy assessment of the results of the third democratization wave, there are already situations in Latin America in which the emergence of the informed citizen, that wishes to deliberate, is a palpable reality. It would be utopian and "culturalistic," in the bad sense of the word, to hinder attempts at institutional reengineering, such as the proposal for a semi-presidentialism or the rebirth of a more authentic parliamentarism, in the name of a reactionary *Volksgeist* that would condemn the region to the old Iberian tradition, no longer prevalent in Spain or Portugal. It would be equally meaningless to dream about an immersion in the spirit of citizen democracy of the dawn of the American Republic. Our democracy is contemporary to mass society, to the Internet, to television, and to the rising concern about social solidarity. We cannot pretend to ground it on possessive individualism nor allow it to be swallowed by the collective, by the state, the trade union, or the all-powerful party.

One might say à la Hegel that, contrary to the American democracy, the moral foundation of freedom for Latin Americans resided in the state that was expected to uphold it. The innovation in contemporary political phenomenon is being driven by emerging forces and values that do not ground politics only on the state. Without embedding democracy in what is alien to us or at least nonconsensual—possessive individualism and the idea of the sovereignty of the free individual as the foundation of the democratic contract—we must reinvent practices and nurture values that safeguard what is fundamental: the freedoms, the legal rights, the sense of the quest for substantive as well as formal equality under the law and the commitment to the common good. This commitment can only serve as the foundation for the democratic belief if it becomes part of the everyday political process, going beyond the mere rhetorical level. The undertaking to expand opportunities and reduce inequalities cannot be grounded only on the moral individual impulse driven by a sense of solidarity. It withers away when it does not find concrete support in public policies and does not result in government action. It must thus transcend the forces of the market as a driver to achieve equality. On the other side, the tradition of a paternal, powerful state is to be replaced by a state open to dialogue and partnership with civil society, withstanding its pressures and being responsive to them in a new context that goes beyond the binary vision of "state or individual," "market or state."

If we stick only with the scaffolding or even the institutional architecture of democracy, no matter how much we perfect the institutions, we will not fill the void, the malaise that today pervades politics. It moves back and forth between the preponderance of the market as the sole regulator of society and the authoritarian arbitrariness of presidents that confound democracy with popular consultations. In this case, the assumption is that the "political will"—by those in power—is enough to produce the nation's happiness (equality and everything else). From the market, on the other hand, one can expect rationality in the allocation of resources and generation of profits, but not the solution to inequalities and social problems. To reinvigorate the electoral laws and the sense of representation, to enforce the rule of law regardless of the social and political status of the person involved, to create mechanisms of participation that go beyond the constant appeal to referenda and do not circumscribe democracy to the congressional but expand the spaces for participative deliberation, and above all, to insist on the fundamental values of freedom and equality, such is the beautiful challenge that we have ahead of us.

A second comment is related to my previous remark about corporativism. There was a time when this theme was high on the academic and political agenda. The works of Philippe Schmitter called special attention to it. Schmitter questioned the old notion of corporativism as something linked only to the state—in Manoilescu's fashion—and showed that there was a societal corporativism. In his debate with the defenders of pluralism as the underpinning of democracy, Schmitter stressed the fact that workers' interests were protected in highly corporative regimes, such as Perón in Argentina and Vargas in Brazil. Hence it is important not to equate corporativism with elitism and perhaps not even reduce all forms of corporativism to fascism or authoritarianism. In this case, the corporation's interest, and also the trade union's, is subordinated to the state that, in the name of the national interest, "suppresses" the class conflicts and rules the economy and the nation.

After so many years, at the apogee of Third Wave democratization in Latin America, I deem it appropriate to revisit some of these old concerns. It is indeed surprising how in presently democratic situations, such as in Brazil or Mexico, to mention some of the more significant—without forgetting about Argentina or Uruguay—with repeated electoral experiences, freedom of press and all the democratic paraphernalia, the corporative connections retain their force while the liberal spirit remains weak. If the political parties, as mentioned above, seem fragile and the interest groups active, the corporative connections (not to be confounded, as Schmitter has shown, with interest groups or lobbies), on the contrary, remain strong.

To prove this point it is enough to look at the proportion of a national congress's agenda occupied with the discussion of laws related to the interests of public servants, state enterprises, trade unions, or professional associations, in the past called "liberal." But it is important not to mix up these corporative forms with the old, fascist-style, corporatist authoritarianism. These are phenomena of a different social and political nature, as duly noted by Schmitter. In the 1970s, at the heyday of the Brazilian military regime that could not be technically defined as fascist, I wrote an article about what I called the "bureaucratic rings," the interest groups organized in networks linking sectors of the public apparatus with sectors of civil society. It seemed to me that "politics," at that time, did not flow through the political parties but rather through these hybrid forms that connected the state with society in a moment in which party life was suffocated by authoritarianism.

What is salient today is the permanence of this type of network even after the democratic rebirth. To put it clearly: one cannot understand some of the Latin American societies based exclusively on a state–civil society dichotomy as if each of these poles inhabited a separate ontological region, when in fact they are interconnected. There is a complex and variable chain linking the traditional forms of civil society organization (parties, nongovernmental organizations, religions, trade unions, etc.) with the corporative-bureaucratic connections. Even the new forms of civil society organization, the nongovernmental organizations, are increasingly and surprisingly becoming interconnected with governmental agencies. Moreover, their use by governments, unions, and parties is something that deserves analysis and evaluation so that we can reframe the very concepts that underpin contemporary democratic politics, insofar as it would be abusive not to consider these processes as part of the redemocratization drive.

I do not say this to minimize the importance of civil society pressure over the state or to negate its relative autonomy, much less to diminish the importance, reiterated above, of revitalizing the political parties. The question is, up to what point will the future of democracy depend upon a reexamination of the traditional forms of representation and an inclusion, in a modified way, of links with a corporative flavor that in the past were rejected by liberal democracy? And won't the corporativism of the great capitalist companies, which are bureaucratizing themselves, affect politics in the very "mature democracies"?

In the case of Latin America, parallel to the permanence or renewal of the forms of corporative connection in countries that have democratized themselves, there are other trends in progress, some of them raising risks to the pursuit of the democratic order. I am obviously referring to the recent political developments in Venezuela, with its regional repercussions. Many analysts see in these events a populist resurgence, but I think that there is more to it. There are populisms that do not attempt to expand the state control over economic production. Indeed, what we are witnessing is a strengthening of authoritarian statism, based on a style of political mobilization which, in order to be grounded on more than just the charisma of the leader, tends to reinforce the corporativism in trade unions and large state-owned companies, as well as to go back to old forms of political mobilization based on a party "of the revolution." This indeed corresponds more closely to a relapse into the type of authoritarian corporativism and political mobilization prevalent in the 1930s and '40s.

In the first case—the existence of corporative connections within political parties and civil society's associational life—we would be seeing an adaptation of elements from the past to conform in a reframed way to the challenges of the democratic present. In the second case, we may well be confronted with a return to or recreation of practices, values, and ideologies that are incompatible with any type of democracy. What gives a charm of novelty to these contemporary attempts to craft a path toward a "heterodox democracy" is the *anti* rhetoric: anti-globalization, anti-Americanism. This rhetoric inflames the minds and hearts of the nostalgic anti-imperialist Left with a fresh breath of hope of "another development," economic and political. Even setting aside the cases of heterodox relapse, the complexity of today's political life calls for more research and new analyses.

In the case of Brazil, for instance, where there is an unquestionable prevalence of the fundamental rules of democracy (civil and political liberties, free press, autonomous courts, freedom of political association, fair and regular elections, periodic shifts in power, etc.), it is intriguing to perceive in the present government a fusion between party interest and public apparatus. And, at the same time, the strength of the market, especially the finance sector and the large capitalist corporations, establishes unexpected connections between different segments of economic life and public activity. Just one example: the pension funds, in Brazil and in any modern democracy, play a crucial role in capital accumulation and in making production and markets more dynamic. Large pension funds were constituted—decades ago—in the Brazilian government-owned enterprises. These have always had among their shareholders significant proportions of private capital. Their shares are traded on the stock exchange—some are blue chips —and they offer American Depositary Receipts (ADRs) in the New York Stock Exchange. The capital accumulated by the pension funds of government-owned enterprises is very significant. When it was invested in the market, the pension funds gained control or influence over many large companies, for example some of those in the mining and telecommunications sector, and hundreds more. All of this is quite natural and occurs in all the world's capitalist economies, but Brazil has a distinctive element: the influence of one party, namely the Workers' Party (PT, which is in power), is decisive on the board of the major pension funds.

Can there be a more telling example of a nonlinear linkage between market and politics, private companies and great bureaucratic corporations and, far from people's awareness, of government and party influence in economic decisions that affect capitalist expansion? In the intersection among these different levels of society, one can find both the principles of perfect competition—consistent with the democratic-capitalist rationale—and the political and partisan criteria and corporatist connections. This challenges linear or simplistic thinking's capacity to describe the situation created by these processes and to foresee behaviors and consequences. If that is the case in Brazil, what then to say about what is happening in Russia?

I will limit myself to these quick considerations to underline how timely this book is and why it is called *Democracies in Danger.* Democracy is assuming so many shapes and undergoing so many metamorphoses in today's world that perhaps it is time to acknowledge that our concept of what democracy is has not evolved to the point of being able to account for contemporary situations. In some countries, transition was incomplete and democracy collapsed. In these cases, it is better to stop qualifying them as undemocratic and search for the best way, without repeating concepts born in other historical contexts, to define the emerging political systems, while refusing to qualify them as democracies.

Equal attention must be paid to the emergence of new practices and values that express and promote a civic culture of participation and responsibility. Informed citizens, active public opinion, and expansion of the public spaces of deliberation are key drivers of the "democratic spirit" in the twenty-first century's open societies. Even acknowledging the existence of traces of a renewed corporativism, there may not be an excluding incompatibility between them and today's forms of democracy. In mass societies, great bureaucratic organizations, be they public or private, with their retinue of corporative interests, may coexist with a vibrant civil society, provided that the instituted political form ensures the space for the discussion of the general interest and that a climate of freedom prevails, in which plural and even contradictory opinions and interests are able to flourish. This is, in any case, the best bet, the only one that can preserve the essence of democracy.

Notes

INTRODUCTION: UNDERTHEORIZED POLITICAL PROBLEMS IN THE FOUNDING DEMOCRATIZATION LITERATURE

1. See Guillermo O'Donnell, Phillippe C. Schmitter, and Laurence Whitehead, eds., *Transitions from Authoritarian Rule* (Baltimore: Johns Hopkins University Press, 1986).

2. See Robert D. Putnam, *Making Democracy Work: Civic Tradition in Modern Italy* (Princeton, N.J.: Princeton University Press, 1993). In his later work, especially his book *Bowling Alone: The Collapse and Revival of American Community* (New York: Simon and Schuster, 2000), he distinguishes between "bonding within groups" and "bridging between groups."

3. Sheri Berman, "Civil Society and the Collapse of the Weimar Republic," *World Politics* 49 (April 1997): 401–29.

4. See his *Ethnic Conflict and Civic Life: Hindus and Muslims in India* (New Haven, Conn.: Yale University Press, 2002).This book received the 2002 Gregory Luebbert Prize for the best book in comparative politics from the American Political Science Association.

5. He also includes an analysis of strife-torn Sri Lanka, with its Buddhist majority and large Hindu and smaller Muslim minorities.

6. For example, writing fourteen years after the "abertura" (the beginnings of a democratic opening) had started in Brazil, I noted that there were hundreds of excellent articles and books on civil society, a score on political society, and almost none on the state security apparatus, especially the police, intelligence, or even the military. See my *Rethinking Military Politics: Brazil and the Southern Cone* (Princeton, N.J.: Princeton University Press, 1988), 4–12.

7. We were meeting at the Cortes (Spain's parliament) in November 2004, within blocks of the location of the March 11, 2004, bombings at the Atocha Railway Station, which killed 191 people.

8. Some of the foundational literature he cites for this shift includes Lau-

rence Whitehead's chapter entitled "On Citizen Security," in his *Democratization: Theory and Experience* (Oxford: Oxford University Press, 2002); and Rob McRae, Donald Hubert, and Lloyd Axworthy, eds., *Human Security and the New Diplomacy: Protecting People, Promoting Peace* (Montreal: McGill-Queens University Press, 2001).

9. Agüero says the "security sector" reform approach originally grew out of British policy circles interested in a holistic approach to development assistance in postconflict situations where good governance, sustainable development, and complete security sector reform were seen as closely interconnected. For some of the literature on this approach to security sector reform, the scholars of which are now beginning to produce journals that will be of interest to democratization specialists, see Robin Luckham, "Democratic Strategies for Security in Transition and Conflict," in *Governing Insecurity: Democratic Control of Military and Security Establishments in Transitional Democracies*, ed. Gavin Cawthra and Robin Luckham (London: Zed Books, 2003). Also see Laurie Nathan, "Obstacles to Security Sector Reform in New Democracies," *Journal of Security Sector Management* 2, no. 3 (September 2004); and Chris Smith, "Security-Sector Reform: Development Breakthrough or Institutional Engineering?" *Conflict, Security and Development* 1, no. 1 (2001): 5–20.

10. I develop and defend this assertion in the introduction to my *Arguing Comparative Politics* (Oxford: Oxford University Press, 2001), 13–17.

11. Also, in the early 1990s, some major scholars such as Giovanni Sartori and Gianfranco Pasquino were beginning to propose "semi-presidentialism" as the best of both worlds of "pure presidentialism" and "pure parliamentarianism." For their arguments, see the chapter by Colton and Skach in this volume.

12. Her book is called *Borrowing Constitutional Designs: Constitutional Law in Weimar Germany and the French Fifth Republic* (Princeton, N.J.: Princeton University Press, 2005).

13. For example, according to Robert Elgie, the editor of *Semi-Presidentialism in Europe* (Oxford: Oxford University Press, 1999), by his classification and current count, sixteen of the twenty-seven European postcommunist countries adopted semi-presidentialism. See his "Variations on a Theme," *Journal of Democracy* 16 (July 2005): 102.

14. In their chapter in this volume, Colton and Skach classify what I call position one, "consolidated majority government," and what I call position two, "divided majority government." I have only used the language of "positions" to facilitate my very compressed exposition of their argument. The useful phrase "electorally generated" was developed by Cindy Skach in *Borrowing Constitutional Designs.*

15. Colton and Skach call this position "divided minority government."

16. For the numerous overlooked mechanisms and conditions—not found

in most semi-presidential systems—that helped produce this result in France, see Alfred Stepan and Ezra N. Suleiman, "The French Fifth Republic: A Model for Import? Reflections on Poland and Brazil," in *Politics, Society, and Democracy: Comparative Studies*, ed. H. E. Chehabi and Alfred Stepan (Boulder, Colo.: Westview Press, 1995), 393–414.This article is reproduced in Stepan, *Arguing Comparative Politics*. The French case is developed in much greater historic detail in Skach, *Borrowing Constitutional Designs*.

17. This assertion is based on Stepan's interview with the former prime minister and president of Portugal, Mário Soares, in Lisbon in June 1998; on Cindy Skach's interview with the president of Poland, Aleksander Kwaśniewski, in Warsaw on May 21, 2001; on Skach and Stepan's long conversations with the former president of Slovenia, Milan Kučan, at our November 2004 Club of Madrid meeting; and on such writings as Leszek Lech Garlicki, "The Presidency in the New Polish Constitution," *East European Constitutional Review* 6 (Spring-Summer 1997): 81–89; and Miro Cerar, "Slovenia," in Elgie, *Semi-Presidentialism in Europe*, 232–59. In 1997 in Poland, as Colton and Skach show, the president and the parliamentary majority, both from the same party, also increased the powers of the constitutional court so as to reduce the autonomy of the president. In Lithuania (unlike Soares, Kwaśniewski, or Kučan), Vytautas Landsbergis, the charismatic but somewhat divisive nationalist independence leader who served as chairman of the Lithuanian parliament and as its acting president, would have liked expanded powers. The voters did not share this desire. His May 1992 referendum on expanded presidential powers failed due to low turnout, and Landsbergis' increased unpopularity and the worsening economic situation eventually forced him to withdraw from the first presidential elections the following year. The first president of newly independent Croatia, Franjo Tudjman (1990–99), expanded his special powers to such a degree that at his death in 1999, Croatia was a super-presidential semi-presidential polity. In the elections for a new president in February 2000, Stjepan Mesić ran on a platform pledging to support a constitutional amendment reducing presidential powers if he were elected and allowing parliament to shape the process. These arguments helped him defeat Dražen Budiša and win the second round. Having gained a parliamentary majority prior to the presidential elections, the coalition that defeated Tudjman's Croatian Democratic Union Party (HDZ) passed constitutional amendments reducing presidential and increasing parliamentary powers with Mesić's support. Mesić was reelected president in January 2005, partly because he had honored his pledge.

18. But as the former prime minister of Portugal, Aníbal Cavaco Silva, stressed at our assembly, a prime minister with a majority in Portugal is not as free from the head of state as a prime minister in a purely parliamentary system would be, because in Portugal, the president without a majority in Par-

liament still had powers to dissolve the Parliament and call elections in order to try to get a majority. Within months this had actually happened in Portugal. Steven D. Roper, on his combined score of presidential powers, gives France a 5, Slovenia less, at 3, and Lithuania a 1. See his "Are All Semipresidential Regimes the Same? A Comparison of Premier-Presidential Regimes," *Comparative Politics* 34 (April 2002): 253–72.

CHAPTER 1: CIVIL SOCIETY, ISLAM, AND ETHNOCOMMUNAL CONFLICT

An earlier version of this chapter was presented at the Club of Madrid general assembly, November 2004. I am grateful to conference participants, an anonymous reader, and Alfred Stepan for their comments on two earlier drafts.

1. While research on the last three countries is currently under way, my work on Hindu-Muslim relations in India is already published: *Ethnic Conflict and Civic Life: Hindus and Muslims in India*. (New Haven, Conn.: Yale University Press, 2002). Wherever the discussion in this chapter focuses on India, I will rely heavily on my book.

2. In single-party systems, political parties are appendages of the state and cannot easily perform civil society functions. In multiparty polities, ruling parties may become part of the state institutions but opposition parties do not, which allows them to be important players in the non-state realm of public activities.

3. The data set was put together in collaboration with Steven Wilkinson (University of Chicago).

4. Ashutosh Varshney, Rizal Panggabean, and Mohammed Zulfan Tadjoeddin, "Creating Datasets in Information-Poor Environments: Patterns of Collective Violence in Indonesia (1990–2003)," *Journal of East Asian Studies* 8, no. 3 (September 2008). Also see Ashutosh Varshney, "Analyzing Collective Violence in Indonesia: An Overview," in the same issue.

5. For the United States, see Stanley Lieberson and Arnold Silverman, "The Precipitants and Underlying Conditions of Race Riots," *American Sociological Review* (December 1965); and for Northern Ireland, Michael Poole, "Geographical Location of Political Violence in Northern Ireland," in *Political Violence: Ireland in Comparative Perspective*, ed. John Darby, Nicholas Dodge, and A. C. Hepburn (Belfast: Appletree Press, 1990).

6. Robert Kaplan, *Balkan Ghosts: A Journey through History* (New York: St. Martin's Press, 1993).

7. Ashutosh Varshney, "Nationalism, Ethnic Conflict, and Rationality," *Perspectives on Politics* (March 2003).

8. Benedict Anderson, *Imagined Communities* (London: Verso Press, 1982).

9. Colley, *Britons* (New Haven, Conn.: Yale University Press, 1991).

10. For a fuller discussion of these gaps, see Ashutosh Varshney, "Ethnicity and Ethnic Conflict" in *Oxford Handbook of Comparative Politics*, ed. Carles Boix and Susan Stokes (New York: Oxford University Press, 2007).

11. Ernest Gellner, *Nations and Nationalism* (Oxford: Blackwell, 1983).

12. For example, the arguments about conflict in Horowitz were based on the commonalities principle. Donald Horowitz, *Ethnic Groups in Conflict* (Berkeley: University of California Press, 1985). In his more recent work, Horowitz has taken note of variance and dealt with it. See Horowitz, *The Deadly Ethnic Riot* (Berkeley: University of California Press, 2001), chap. 12.

13. Gary King, Robert Keohane, and Sidney Verba, *Designing Social Inquiry* (Princeton, N.J.: Princeton University Press, 1994).

14. For details, see the following exchange between Varshney and Laitin: Ashutosh Varshney, "Recognizing the Tradeoffs We Make," and David Laitin, "Ethnography and/or Rational Choice," both in *Qualitative Methods* 4, no. 1 (Spring 2006).

15. The cities were Aligarh and Calicut, Hyderabad and Lucknow, and Ahmedabad and Surat.

16. Robert Putnam, *Bowling Alone: The Collapse and Revival of American Community* (New York: Simon and Schuster, 2000).

17. Whether custody rights should be determined on the basis of the *shariat* or civil law if the husband converted to Islam from Hinduism just before filing for divorce was a much discussed and contentious issue in Malay-Indian relations in 2007.

18. For an analysis of how this battle has evolved in favor of moderate Muslims in Malaysia, whereas it went in the direction of extremism in Pakistan, see S. Val Reza Nasr, *The Islamic Leviathan* (Oxford: Oxford University Press, 2001).

19. Laskar Jihad has openly admitted participating in Maluku riots. See Noorhaidi Hasan, "Faith and Politics: The Rise of Laskar Jihad in the Era of Transition in Indonesia," *Indonesia* 73 (2002): 145–69.

20. Varshney, Panggabean, and Tadjoeddin, "Creating Datasets."

21. For details, see Douglas Ramage, *Politics in Indonesia: Democracy, Islam and the Ideology of Tolerance* (London: Routledge, 1995).

22. Cited in ibid., 64.

23. Alfred Stepan, "The World's Religious System and Democracy: Crafting the Twin Tolerations," in *Arguing Comparative Politics* (Oxford: Oxford University Press, 2001).

24. For a remarkable first-person account, see Narendra Jadhav, *Untouchables: My Family's Triumphant Journey out of the Caste System in Modern India* (New York: Scribner, 2005).

25. Nathan Glazer, *We Are All Multiculturalists Now* (Cambridge, Mass.: Harvard University Press, 1996).

26. James Fearon and David Laitin, "Explaining Inter-Ethnic Cooperation," *American Political Science Review* (December 1996).

27. The awful riots in Gujarat state in 1969 are an example of such behavior. See Varshney, *Ethnic Conflict*, chaps. 10 and 11.

28. State involvement in the 1983 riots of Sri Lanka is now widely accepted. Indeed, during her tenure, Chandrika Kumaratunga, president of Sri Lanka from 1994 to 2005, explicitly apologized for the role of the state in the 1983 violence. For a well-known analysis prompted by these riots, see Stanley Tambiah, *Sri Lanka: Ethnic Fratricide and the Dismantling of Democracy* (Chicago: University of Chicago Press, 1991).

29. For further details, see Ashutosh Varshney, "Understanding Gujarat Violence," *Items and Issues*, Newsletter of the Social Science Research Council, New York (Fall 2002).

30. This is based on a close reading of the following newspapers: the *Times of India*; the *Indian Express*; and the *Hindustan Times*.

31. "Parivar Wars," *Times of India*, June 26, 2002.

32. There was a Malay-Indian riot, however, in 1998.

33. Manjit Singh Sidhu, *Kuala Lumpur and Its Population* (Kuala Lumpur: Surindar Publications, 1978), 21. Also see C. G. Clarke and M. S. Sidhu, "Racial Segregation in Peninsular Malaysian Towns," *Geographical Journal* 143 (1977).

34. James Jesudason, "State Legitimacy, Minority Political Participation, and Ethnic Conflict in Indonesia and Malaysia," in *Social Cohesion and Conflict Prevention in Asia*, ed. Nat J. Colletta, Teck Ghee Lim, and Anita Kelles-Viitanen (Washington D.C.: World Bank, 2001).

35. "Workers of the Same Race Stick Together," *Straits Times*, February 1, 2003. Given the rising Malay-Indian tensions in Malaysia, it is not clear how well this policy has been implemented or is working.

36. Suresh Khopade, *Bhiwandi Riots and After*, unpublished manuscript, preface.

37. Ibid., 115.

38. The citations in this paragraph are from ibid., 116.

39. Both citations in this paragraph from ibid., 118

40. Ibid., 119.

41. Usha Thakkar, "Mohalla Committees of Bombay: Candles in Ominous Darkness," *Economic and Political Weekly*, February 7, 2004.

42. For Latin American materials on corporatism, see Alfred Stepan, *State and Society: Peru in Comparative Perspective* (Princeton, N.J.: Princeton University Press, 1978); and James Malloy, ed., *Authoritarianism and Corporatism in Latin America* (Pittsburgh: University of Pittsburgh Press, 1977). In a

recent book, Yashar uses the term "corporatist citizenship" to characterize the twentieth-century Latin American organizational model until the neoliberal phase arrived in the 1980s. See Deborah Yashar, *Contesting Citizenship in Latin America* (New York: Cambridge University Press, 2005).

43. For how the self-management industrial societies of Tito's Yugoslavia fared, see Sharon Zukin, *Beyond Marx and Tito* (New York: Cambridge University Press, 1975); and Ellen Comisso, *Workers' Control under Plan and Market: Implications of Yugoslavia's Self-Management* (New York: Cambridge University Press, 1979).

44. See the recent empirical arguments in Donald Rothchild and Philip Roeder, "Power Sharing as an Impediment to Peace and Democracy," and "Dilemmas of Power Sharing in Divided Societies," in *Sustainable Peace* (Ithaca, N.Y.: Cornell University Press, 2005).

CHAPTER 2: DEBATING SECESSION PEACEFULLY AND DEMOCRATICALLY

1. These issues are fully explored in a series of short monographs, *The Canadian Democratic Audit,* published by the University of British Columbia Press under the editorship of William Cross.

2. The phrase is Charles Taylor's. See John Erik Fossum, "Deep Diversity versus Constitutional Patriotism," *Ethnicities* 1 (2001): 179–206.

3. And indeed, since the British conquest of New France a century earlier, the British permitted the *Canadiens* to maintain their language, Roman Catholic religion, and system of civil law.

4. For a thorough analysis of these three dimensions of diversity, see Will Kymlicka, *Finding Our Way: Rethinking Ethnocultural Relations in Canada* (Toronto: Oxford University Press, 1998).

5. The story is well-told in Peter Russell, *Constitutional Odyssey: Can Canadians Become a Sovereign People?* 3rd ed. (Toronto: University of Toronto Press, 2004).

6. For a full discussion of the federal position in this debate, and an exchange of correspondence between Stéphane Dion, the federal minister of Intergovernmental Affairs, and Lucien Bouchard, the PQ premier of Quebec, see Dion, ed. *Straight Talk: Speeches and Writings on Canadian Unity* (Montreal: McGill-Queen's University Press, 1999).

7. *Reference re the Secession of Quebec* [1998] 2 S.C.R.

8. For comment on the judgment see David Schneiderman, ed., *The Quebec Decision: Perspective on the Supreme Court Ruling on Secession* (Toronto: James Lorimer, 1999).

9. Canada, *Clarity Act* 2000. c.26.

10. See Keith G. Banting, Roger Gibbins, Peter M. Leslie, Alain Noel,

Richard Simeon, and Robert Young. *Open Federalism: Interpretation, Significance* (Kingston, Canada: Institute of Intergovernmental Relations, 2006).

11. The Bloc Québécois, the federal arm of the secessionists was briefly the largest opposition in Parliament, with the ironic title of "Her Majesty's Loyal Opposition."

12. For examples of such thinking in English Canada, see Richard Simeon, ed. *Must Canada Fail?* (Montreal: McGill-Queen's University Press, 1977); and David Cameron, ed., *The Referendum Papers: Essays on Secession and National Unity* (Toronto: University of Toronto Press, 1999).

13. Asymmetrical federalism refers to a pattern in which one (or more) states or provinces exercises powers and responsibilities not exercised by the others. Asymmetry may either be formally enshrined in the constitution or be de facto in the practice of intergovernmental relations. There is little asymmetry in the Canadian Constitution but considerable asymmetry in practice.

14. See Tony Hill, "Variability of Support for Sovereignty in Quebec," paper presented to the Midwest Political Science Association, Chicago, 2005.

15. For example, Alain-G. Gagnon and Francois Rocher, "Presentation," in *Repliques au détracteurs de la souverainëté du Québec* (Montréal, vlb éditeur, 1992). For a sympathetic, but more skeptical view, see Jeremy Webber, "Just How Civic Is Civic Nationalism in Quebec?" in *Citizenship, Diversity and Pluralism: Canadian and Comparative Perspectives*, ed. Alan Cairns, John C. Courtney, Peter Mackinnon, Hans J. Michelmann, and David E. Smith (Montreal: McGill-Queen's University Press, 2000), 87–107.

16. This bargain was enshrined in the *Quebec Act* (1774 Geo III, c.83). The act was partly designed to dissuade French-Canadians from joining the American revolutionaries and was denounced in the American colonies as one of the Intolerable Acts of the British Parliament that justified U.S. independence.

17. S. M. Lipset somewhat controversially traces out the implications of the revolutionary and counterrevolutionary traditions of the United States and Canada in his *Continental Divide: The Values and Institutions of the United States and Canada* (New York: Routledge, Chapman, and Hall, 1992).

18. For an analysis of the dynamics of intergovernmental relations in Canada, see Richard Simeon, *Federal-Provincial Diplomacy: The Making of Recent Policy in Canada* (Toronto: University of Toronto Press, 1971; reissued with a new postscript, 2006).

19. Ronald L. Watts, *Comparing Federal Systems*, 2nd ed. (Montreal: McGill-Queen's University Press, 1999), 113.

20. See Richard Simeon and Daniel Patrick Conway, "Federalism and the Management of Conflict in Divided Societies," in *Multinational Democracies*, ed. Alain-G. Gagnon and James Tully (Cambridge: Cambridge University Press, 2001), 338–65.

21. For a full discussion of this debate, see John McGarry, Brendan O'Leary, and Richard Simeon, "Integration or Accommodation? The Enduring Debate in Conflict Regulation," in *Constitutional Design for Divided Societies: Integration or Accommodation?* ed. Sujit Choudhry (Oxford: Oxford University Press, 2008), 41–90.

22. This is the classic Lijphart-Horowitz debate. See, for example, chapters by Arend Lijphart and Donald Horowitz in *The Architecture of Democracy: Constitutional Design, Conflict Management and Democracy,* ed. Andrew Reynolds (Oxford: Oxford University Press, 2002): Horowitz, "Constitutional Design," 15–36, and Lijphart, "Wave of Power-Sharing," 37–54.

23. This is despite the fact that the court is appointed by the federal government. Three of the nine justices must be from the Quebec bar.

24. Peter H. Russell describes the Canadian Supreme Court decision on the federal government's attempt to make constitutional change without substantial provincial consent in 1980 as "bold statescraft based on questionable jurisprudence." Peter Russell, ed., *The Court and the Constitution: Comments on the Supreme Court Reference on Constitutional Amendment, 1982* (Kingston, Canada: Institute of Intergovernmental Relations, 1982).

25. See Harvey Lazar, "Non-constitutional Renewal: Toward a New Equilibrium in the Federation," in *Canada: The State of the Federation 1997: Non-constitutional Renewal* (Montreal: McGill-Queen's University Press, 1998).

26. David Cameron and Richard Simeon, eds., *Language Matters: Pathways of Association in Canadian Voluntary Associations* (Vancouver: University of British Columbia Press, 2008).

CHAPTER 3: THE NEW "DOUBLE CHALLENGE"

1. Guillermo O'Donnell spoke of the "slow death" of democracy in which there is a "progressive diminution of existing spaces for the exercise of civilian power and the effectiveness of the classic guarantees of liberal constitutionalism." "Transitions, Continuities, and Paradoxes," in *Issues in Democratic Consolidation: The New South American Democracies in Comparative Perspective,* ed. Scott Mainwaring, Guillermo O'Donnell, and J. Samuel Valenzuela (Notre Dame, Ind.: University of Notre Dame Press, 1992).

2. Arturo Valenzuela's "Latin America's Interrupted Presidencies"—his contribution to this volume—maintains that while "in the past the military was at the heart of the problem . . . Latin American militaries no longer mix openly in politics." However, he asserts that "instability remains a persistent problem and sometimes proceeds along lines that are eerily reminiscent of the past," with the military sometimes participating in the process of interrupting presidencies. He finds the source of that process in the regional features of presidentialism.

3. Vladimir Putin's institutional reform to strengthen the state's response to terrorism has been a good example of this. See "Putin Issues Plan to Tighten Grasp, Citing Terrorism: Overhaul of Political System—Opponents Call It Step Back," *New York Times*, Tuesday, September 14, 2004, A1. Those kinds of political reform vastly overshadow and subsume any specific threats to democracy coming from the armed forces or other state security agencies.

4. Alfred Stepan, *Rethinking Military Politics: Brazil and the Southern Cone* (Princeton, N.J.: Princeton University Press, 1988).

5. For postconflict democracies, see Gavin Cawthra and Robin Luckham, eds., *Governing Insecurity: Democratic Control of Military and Security Establishments in Transitional Democracies* (London: Zed Books, 2003).

6. See Philippe C. Schmitter, "Transitology: the Science or the Art of Democratization?" in *The Consolidation of Democracy in Latin America*, ed. Joseph S. Tulchin with Bernice Romero (Boulder, Colo.: Lynne Rienner, 1995).

7. Maryann K. Cusimano, *Beyond Sovereignty: Issues for a Global Agenda* (Boston: St. Martin's, 2000); Michael C. Desch, Jorge I. Domínguez, and Andrés Serbín, eds. *From Pirates to Drug Lords: The Post–Cold War Caribbean Security Environment* (Albany: State University of New York Press, 1998).

8. The concept of security sector reform developed in policy circles in relation to development assistance, pointing out the link between good governance, sustainable development, and the security sector (including the armed forces, paramilitary groups, intelligence units, and the police). See Chris Smith, "Security-sector Reform: Development Breakthrough or Institutional Engineering?" *Conflict, Security and Development* 1, no.1 (2001): 5–20; Nicole Ball, "Transforming Security Sectors: The IMF and World Bank Approaches," *Conflict, Security and Development* 1, no. 1 (2001): 45–66; Laurie Nathan, "Obstacles to Security Sector Reform in New Democracies," *Journal of Security Sector Management* 2, no. 3 (2004), www.ssronline.org/jofssm/issues/jofssm_0203_nathan.pdf?CFID=1208258&CFTOKEN=36427793; and Robin Luckham, "Democratic Strategies for Security in Transition and Conflict," in Cawthra and Luckham, *Governing Insecurity*.

9. See the proposal for a human security doctrine for Europe by a study group convened by Mary Kaldor: "A Human Security Doctrine for Europe," The Barcelona Report of the Study Group on Europe's Security Capabilities, Presented to the European Union High Representative for Common Foreign and Security Policy, Javier Solana, Barcelona, September 15, 2004. See also Rob McRae, Don Hubert, and Lloyd Axworthy, eds., *Human Security and the New Diplomacy: Protecting People, Promoting Peace* (Montreal: McGill-Queen's University Press, 2001); and Miriam Kornblith, "Human Security: Definition and Challenges for Latin America and the Caribbean," in *Human Security, Conflict Prevention and Peace*, ed. Moufida Goucha and Francisco

Rojas Aravena (Santiago: UNESCO-FLACSO-Chile, 2003). On citizen security, see Laurence Whitehead, *Democratization: Theory and Experience* (Oxford: Oxford University Press, 2002), chap. 7.

10. Felipe Agüero, "Legacies of Transitions: Institutionalization, the Military, and Democracy in South America," *Mershon International Studies Review* 42, no. 2 (1998): 383–404.

11. Wendy Hunter, *Eroding Military Influence in Brazil: Politicians against Soldiers* (Chapel Hill: University of North Carolina Press, 1997); Jorce Zaverucha, *FHC, forcas armadas e policia: Entre o autoritarismo e a democracia* (Rio de Janeiro: Record, 2005); and Jorge Zaverucha, "La militarizacion de la seguridad publica en Brasil," *Nueva Sociedad,* no. 213 (2008).

12. Felipe Agüero, "Democratización y militares: Balance de diecisiete años desde la transición," in *Chile: Política y modernización democrática,* ed. Manuel Alcántara and Leticia M. Ruiz Rodríguez (Barcelona: Edicions Bellatera, 2006).

13. See Narcís Serra, *La transicion militar: Reflexiones en torno a la reforma democratica de las fuerzas armadas* (Barcelona: Debate, 2008).

14. Muthiah Alagappa, ed. *Coercion and Governance: The Declining Political Role of the Military in Asia* (Stanford, Calif.: Stanford University Press, 2001).

15. John Bailey and Jorge Chabat, eds., *Transnational Crime and Public Security: Challenges to Mexico and the United States* (Berkeley: University of California Press, 2002); Oscar Rocha, "Civil Military Relations and Security Policy in Mexico," CSIS Mexico Project, September 10, 2003.

16. Michael Bratton and Nicolas van de Walle, *Democratic Experiments in Africa: Regime Transitions in Comparative Perspective* (Cambridge: Cambridge University Press, 1997).

17. J. 'Kayode Fayemi, "Governing the Security Sector in a Democratising Polity: Nigeria," in Gavin Cawthra and Robin Luckham, *Governing Insecurity.*

18. While in many cases the military owns businesses that support its spending, it is also relevant that top military elites are routinely incorporated into the board of large firms. Harold Crouch, "Civil-Military Relations in Southeast Asia," in *Consolidating Third Wave Democracies: Themes and Perspectives,* ed. Larry Diamond, Marc F. Plattner, Yun-han Chu, and Hung-mao Tien (Baltimore: Johns Hopkins University Press, 1997). See also Geoffrey Robinson, "Indonesia: On a New Course?"; and James Ockey, "Thailand: The Struggle to Redefine Civil-Military Relations," both in M. Alagappa, *Coercion and Governance.* For Latin America, see Rut Diamint, *Democracia y seguridad en América Latina* (Buenos Aires: Grupo Editor Latinoamericano, 2001); and Arnoldo Brenes and Kevin Casas, *Soldados como ermpresarios: Los negocios de los militares en centroamérica* (San José, Costa Rica: Fundación Arias Para la Paz, 1998).

19. Robin Luckham, "Democratic Strategies."

20. Ibid., 18.

21. Peter Feaver, *Armed Servants: Agency, Oversight, and Civil-Military Relations* (Cambridge, Mass.: Harvard University Press, 2003).

22. Ibid. Brazil also has been a good example: see Paulo de Mesquita Neto, "From Intervention to Participation: The Transformation of Military Politics in Brazil, 1974–1992" (PhD diss., Columbia University, 1995); and Eliézer Rizzo de Oliveira, "O papel das forças armadas na nova constituição e no futuro da democracia no Brasil," *Vozes* 82, no. 2 (1988).

23. Peter D. Feaver and Richard H. Kohn, eds. *Soldiers and Civilians: The Civil-Military Gap and American National Security* (Cambridge, Mass.: MIT Press, 2001).

24. See Narcís Serra's review of the literature in his *La transicion militar.*

25. See Felipe Agüero, *Soldiers, Civilians, and Democracy: Post-Franco Spain in Comparative Perspective* (Baltimore: Johns Hopkins University Press, 1995), and Narcís Serra, *La transicion militar,* and his contribution to this volume.

26. Argentina, for instance, once hailed for its early pursuit of military reforms, saw many of them remain limited in scope as a result of military pressure and leadership failures. Rut Diamint, *Democracia y seguridad.* See also, Rut Diamint, ed., *Control civil y fuerzas armadas en las nuevas democracias Latinoamericanas* (Buenos Aires: Grupo Editor Latinoamericano, 1999). Taiwan, South Korea, the Philippines and Thailand also are cases of mixed results. M. Alagappa, *Coercion and Governance.* Nigeria and Ghana could go in this list as well. Eboe Hutchful, "Pulling Back from the Brink: Ghana's Experience," in Cawthra and Luckham, *Governing Insecurity.*

27. For recent scholarship on these subjects see Thomas C. Bruneau and Scott D. Tollefson, eds., *Who Guards the Guardians and How: Democratic Civil-Military Relations* (Austin: University of Texas Press, 2006).

28. *Ready, Aim, Foreign Policy,* WOLA Report, March 2008.

29. For Spain, see Agüero, *Soldiers, Civilians, and Democracy.* For east-central Europe, see Harald von Riekhoff, "Introduction," in *The Evolution of Civil-Military Relations in East-Central Europe and the Former Soviet Union,* ed. Natalie L. Mychajlyszyn and Harald von Riekhoff (Westport, Conn.: Praeger 2004). For Africa, see Ann M. Fitzgerald and Anícia Lalá, eds., *Networking the Networks: Supporting Regional Peace and Security Agendas in Africa* (Shrivenham, UK: GFN-SSR, 2001). For Latin America, see Diamint, *Democracia y seguridad.* In his recent research, Arturo Sotomayor found that the benefits of participating in UN-led peacekeeping depend on the extent to which government agencies of participating countries are in fact, and effectively, run by civilians, and on whether participating forces are exposed to armies with a tradition of civilian control. Arturo C. Sotomayor, "The Peace

Soldier from the South: From Praetorianism to Peacekeeping?" (PhD diss., Columbia University, 2004). For a study of unintended effects of peacekeeping, see Michael C. Williams, "Civil-Military Relations and Peacekeeping," Adelphi Paper 321 (London: International Institute for Strategic Studies London, 1998). For an examination of the impact of globalization, democratization, technological innovation, and economic change on civil-military relations, see Thomas C. Bruneau and Harold Trinkunas, eds., *Global Politics of Defense Reform* (New York: Palgrave Macmillan, 2008).

30. Arthur Trindade de Maranhao Costa, *Entre a lei e a ordem* (Rio de Janeiro: FGV, 2004). For a discussion of different ways of understanding police demilitarization and its various aspects, see Arthur Costa and Matheus Medeiros, "Police demilitarisation: Cops, soldiers and democracy," *Conflict, Security and Development* 2, no. 2 (2002).

31. Juan Linz and Alfred Stepan, *Problems of Democratic Transition and Consolidation: Southern Europe, South America and Post-communist Europe* (Baltimore: Johns Hopkins University Press, 1996).

32. Argentine Supreme Court judge Raul Zaffaroni spoke of a rule of police that threatens the rule of law. "No me gusta el autoritarismo cool," *Pagina 12*, August 29, 2004. See also Catalina Smulovitz, "Citizen Insecurity and Fear: Public and Private Responses in Argentina," in *Crime and Violence in Latin America: Citizen Security, Democracy, and the State*, ed. Hugo Frühling, Joseph S. Tulchin, and Heather A. Golding (Baltimore and Washington, D.C.: Johns Hopkins University Press and Woodrow Wilson Center Press, 2003).

33. See Charles Call, "Police Reform, Human Rights and Democratization in Post-Conflict Settings: Lessons from El Salvador," in *Rebuilding Societies after Civil Wars: Critical Roles for International Assistance*, ed. K. Kumar (Boulder, Colo.: Lynne Rienner, 1997). For the way this dilemma played out in Guatemala, see Jennifer Schirmer, "The Guatemalan Politico-Military Project: Whose Ship of State?" in *Political Armies: The Military and Nation Building in the Age of Democracy*, ed. Kees Koonings and Dirk Kuijt (London: Zed Books, 2002).

34. See, for instance, Angelina Snodgrass Godoy, "Lynching and the Democratization of Terror in Postwar Guatemala," *Human Rights Quarterly* 24 (2002): 640–61, and by the same author, "La Muchacha Respondona: Crime and Human Rights in Contemporary Guatemala," paper presented at the Conference on Democracy and Human Rights in Latin America, Center for Latin American Studies, University of Oregon, Eugene, November 5–8, 2003.

35. Claudio Fuentes, "Violent Police, Passive Citizens: The Failure of Societal Accountability in Chile," in *Enforcing the Rule of Law: The Politics of Social Accountability in Latin America*, ed. Enrique Peruzzotti and Catalina Smulovitz (Pittsburgh: University of Pittsburgh Press, 2006).

36. Gino Costa and Carlos Basombrío, *Liderazgo civil en el ministerio del interior: Testimonio de una experiencia de reforma policial y gestión democrática de la seguridad en el perú* (Lima: Instituto de Estudios Peruanos, 2004); and Carlos Basombrío, "The Militarization of Public Security in Peru," in Frühling, Tulchin, and Golding, *Crime and Violence.*

37. Rachel Neild, "From National Security to Citizen Security: Civil Society and the Evolution of Public Order Debates," occasional paper (Montreal: International Center for Human Rights and Democratic Development, 1999).

38. For police reform see Rachel Neild, "Democratic Police Reforms in War-Torn Societies," *Conflict, Security and Development* 1, no. 1 (2001). In the case of Nigeria see Innocent Chukwuma, "Reforming the Nigerian Police: Issues at Stake," in *Providing Security for People: Enhancing Security through Police, Justice, and Intelligence Reform in Africa,* ed. Chris Ferguson and Jeffrey O. Isima (Shrivenham, UK: Global Facilitation Network for Security Sector Reform, 2004).

39. Reform experience in the New York City Police Department has been useful in countering these trends. See Amnesty International, *Police Brutality and Excessive Force in the New York City Police Department* (New York, 1996); and Jerome H. Skolnick and James J. Fyfe, *Above the Law: Police and the Excessive Use of Force* (New York: Free Press, 1993). See also, for South Africa, Themba Masuku, "Numbers that Count: National Monitoring of Police Conduct," *SA Crime Quarterly,* no. 8 (June 2004).

40. Costa and Basombrío, *Liderazgo civil.*

41. Dennis P. Rosenbaum, ed., *The Challenge of Community Policing* (Thousand Oaks, Calif.: Sage, 1994); and Joseph A. Schafer, *Community Policing: The Challenges of Successful Organizational Change* (El Paso, Tex.: LFB Scholarly Publishing, 2001).

42. Mark Shaw, *Crime and Policing in Post-Apartheid South Africa: Transforming under Fire* (Bloomington: Indiana University Press, 2002).

43. Paulo Mesquita Neto and Adriana Loche, "Police Community Partnerships in Brazil," in Frühling, Tulchin, and Golding, *Crime and Violence.* For a review and assessment of police reform in Latin America, see Hugo Frühling, "Police Reform and the Process of Democratization," in *Crime and Violence.* Also, Hugo Frühling, "Policía comunitaria y reforma policial en América Latina: Cuál es el impacto?" Centro de Estudios en Seguridad Ciudadana, Universidad de Chile, Serie Documentos, May 2003.

44. Gavin Cawthra and Robin Luckham, "Democratic Control and the Security Sector: The Scope for Transformation and its Limits," in Cawthra and Luckam, *Governing Insecurity.*

45. For a comprehensive effort at presenting the interrelatedness of military, police, and intelligence problems in the pursuit of democratization and

effectiveness, see FLACSO-Chile, *Reporte del sector seguridad de America Latina y el Caribe* (Santiago, 2007).

46. Anícia Lalá, "Picturing the Landscape: Police, Justice, Penal and Intelligence Reforms in Africa," in Ferguson and Isima, *Providing Security*.

47. Kevin O'Brien, "Controlling the Hydra: An Historical Analysis of South African Intelligence Oversight," conference paper, Geneva Centre for the Democratic Control of Armed Forces, The Norwegian Parliamentary Intelligence Oversight Committee, and the Human Rights Centre, Department of Law, University of Durham, Oslo, September 2003. For an account of the negotiated character of intelligence reforms and their constitutionalization in South Africa, see Sandy Africa, "The Restructuring of the Intelligence Services in South Africa: An Assessment of the Transformation Process," in Ferguson and Isima, *Providing Security*.

48. These features are highlighted in Laurence Lustgarten and Ian Leigh, *In from the Cold: National Security and Parliamentary Democracy* (Oxford: Oxford University Press, 1994), cited in Kieran Williams and Dennis Deletant, *Security Intelligence Services in New Democracies: The Czech Republic, Slovakia, and Romania* (Houndsmills, Hampshire, UK: Palgrave, 2001), 15. See also J. J. Blais, "The Political Accountability of Intelligence Services—Canada," *Intelligence and National Security* 4, no. 1 (1989); and Joseph F. Ryan, "Review of the Canadian Security Intelligence Service: A Suitable Model for the United Kingdom?" *Intelligence and National Security* 5, no. 3 (1990). For a recent and insightful comparative study of intelligence, see Thomas C. Bruneau and Steven C. Boraz, eds., *Reforming Intelligence: Obstacles to Democratic Control and Effectiveness* (Austin: University of Texas Press, 2007).

49. Hans Born, "Democratic and Parliamentary Oversight of the Intelligence Services: Best Practices and Procedures," Working Paper Series—no. 20, Geneva Centre for the Democratic Control of Armed Forces, Geneva, May 2002.

50. Philip B. Heymann, *Terrorism, Freedom, and Security* (Cambridge, Mass.: MIT Press, 2003), 133.

51. James A. Baker and Lee H. Hamilton, *The Iraq Study Group Report: The Way Forward—A New Approach* (Washington, D.C. Filiquarian, 2007).

CHAPTER 4: BEYOND THREATS TO DEMOCRACY FROM THE ARMED FORCES, POLICE, AND INTELLIGENCE

1. This essay is largely based on the personal experience of the author, so it does not have the typical notes found in the other chapters. However, for readers interested in reading further about the Spanish transition, see the chapter on Spain, "The Paradigmatic Case of *Reforma pactada—ruptura pactada*:

Spain," in *Problems of Democratic Transition and Consolidation: Southern Europe, South America, and Post-Communist Europe*, ed. Juan J. Linz and Alfred Stepan (Baltimore: Johns Hopkins University Press, 1996), 87–116. For an extensively documented analysis of the gradual control of the military in the Spanish transition and consolidation, see Felipe Agüero, *Soldiers, Civilians, and Democracy: Post-Franco Spain in Comparative Perspective* (Baltimore: Johns Hopkins University Press, 1995). Spanish-language readers should consult Narcís Serra, *La transición militar: Reflexiones en torno a la reforma democrática de las fuerzas armadas* (Barcelona: Debate, 2008).

CHAPTER 5: LATIN AMERICA'S INTERRUPTED PRESIDENCIES

1. David Scott Palmer, "Peru: Collectively Defending Democracy in the Western Hemisphere," in *Beyond Sovereignty: Collectively Defending Democracy in the Americas*, ed. Tom Farer (Baltimore: Johns Hopkins University Press, 1996), 258.

2. For background, see Jonathan Hartlyn and Arturo Valenzuela, "Democracy in Latin America Since 1930," in *Latin America since 1930: Economy, Society, and Politics*, ed. Leslie Bethel (Cambridge: Cambridge University Press, 1994)

3. Marta Lagos, "A Road with No Return? Latin America's Lost Illusions," *Journal of Democracy* 14 (April 2003): 161–73.

4. A classic study is Charles W. Anderson, *Politics and Economic Change in Latin America* (Princeton, N.J.: Van Norstrand Press, 1967). See also John J. Johnson, *The Military and Society in Latin America* (Stanford, Calif.: Stanford University Press, 1964); and Edwin Lieuwen, *Generals vs. Presidents: Neomilitarism in Latin America* (New York: Praeger, 1964).

5. Alfred Stepan, *The Military in Politics: Changing Patterns in Brazil* (Princeton, N.J.: Princeton University Press, 1971); and Guillermo O'Donnell, *Modernization and Bureaucratic-Authoritarianism: Studies in South American Politics* (Berkeley: University of California Press, 1973).

6. See Farer, *Beyond Sovereignty*, passim.

7. Dankwart A. Rustow, "Transitions to Democracy: Toward a Dynamic Model," *Comparative Politics* 2 (April 1970): 337–63. See also Juan J. Linz and Alfred C. Stepan, *Problems of Democratic Transition and Consolidation* (Baltimore: Johns Hopkins University Press, 1996).

8. Peter Hakim, "Latin America's Lost Illusions: Dispirited Politics," *Journal of Democracy* 14 (April 2003): 121.

9. Anderson, *Politics and Economic Change*, makes this point in describing the continuous crises of presidential democracies in mid-twentieth century.

10. J. Mark Payne et al., *Democracies in Development: Politics and Reform*

in *Latin America* (Washington, D.C.: Inter-American Development Bank, 2002), 74, 211.

11. Juan J. Linz, "Presidential or Parliamentary Democracy: Does It Make a Difference?" in *The Failure of Presidential Democracy*, ed. Juan J. Linz and Arturo Valenzuela (Baltimore: Johns Hopkins University Press, 1994), 18–19. A first draft of this classic essay was written for a conference held at the Woodrow Wilson International Center for Scholars in 1984. More than any other scholar, Juan Linz through his trenchant studies has consistently warned of the shortcomings of presidential democracies.

12. Rafael Caldera, a former president of Venezuela (1969–73) and an architect of the elite agreements that ended authoritarian rule, had an even more negative effect on his party when he succeeded Pérez after the latter's impeachment. Having failed to win the nomination of the party that he had founded, Caldera insisted on running as an independent. Repeat candidacies of former presidents after they have left office are the stuff of legend in Latin American history. The pattern has continued into recent decades, with not only Caldera and Carlos Andres Perez in Venezuela, but figures as dissimilar as Leonel Fernández of the Dominican Republic, Jorge Alessandri of Chile, Alan Garcia of Peru, Hipólito Mejia of the Dominican Republic, Raul Alfonsín and Carlos Saúl Menem of Argentina, and Julio María Sanguinetti of Uruguay.

13. In addition to Linz and Valenzuela, *Failure of Presidential Democracy*, see Juan J. Linz, "The Perils of Presidentialism," *Journal of Democracy* 1 (Winter 1990): 51–69; and Arturo Valenzuela, "Latin America: Presidentialism in Crisis," *Journal of Democracy* 4 (October 1993): 3–16. Critics of these views, while acknowledging the problems with presidentialism, tended to overstate the success of presidential regimes in the early years of democratic transition. See the essays in Scott Mainwaring et al., eds., *Presidentialism and Democracy in Latin America* (New York: Cambridge University Press, 1997).

14. An essential work in the field is Matthew Soberg Shugart and John Carey, *Presidents and Assemblies: Constitutional Design and Electoral Dynamics* (New York: Cambridge University Press, 1992).

15. Linz and Stepan, *Problems of Democratic Transition*, 276–82.

16. Arend Lijphart makes this argument in signaling a preference for parliamentary government. See his "Constitutional Design for Divided Societies," *Journal of Democracy* 15 (April 2004): 102. Linz also has expressed skepticism with semi-presidential formulae.

17. I am indebted to former Portuguese prime minister Antonio Gutiérrez for relaying these insights to me in personal conversation. Arend Lijphart notes that this combination of rules from the German and French parliamentary systems would protect cabinet effectiveness while assuring the parlia-

ment's prerogatives to replace the government with another or force elections. See Lijphart, "Constitutional Design," 104.

18. There is a long tradition of constitutional engineering in Latin America, primarily aimed at softening the winner-take-all tendencies of presidential regimes. These include the adoption of proportional representation electoral systems, plural executives in Uruguay, the National Front in Colombia that sought to apportion power equally between the two main parties, the figure of the prime minister in the Peruvian and Venezuelan Constitutions, and the provision permitting the president to dissolve Congress in the contemporary Uruguayan Constitution. The Cuban Constitution of 1940 had strong parliamentary features. For a classic study, see Karl Lowenstein, "The Balance between Legislative and Executive Power: A Study in Comparative Constitutional Law," *University of Chicago Law Review* 5 (1937–38): 566–608; and William S. Stokes, "Parliamentary Government in Latin America," *American Political Science Review* 39 (June 1945): 522–35. See also Carl J. Friedrich, *Constitutional Government and Democracy: Theory and Practice in Europe and America* (Boston, Mass.: Ginn and Company, 1950).

19. Fundación Milenio was close to the Moviemiento Nacionalista Revolucionario (MNR), then headed by party president Gonzalo Sanchez de Lozada, who championed the initiative of proposing broad constitutional reforms and took a direct personal interest in the commission's deliberations. Support for the work of the commission came from the Konrad Adenauer Foundation and the National Endowment for Democracy. The commission was broadly representative of all political tendencies in Bolivia at the time and included distinguished Bolivian lawyers including Fernando Aguirre, Raúl España, Juan Cristóbal Urioste, and Carlos Hugo Molina. International experts who participated in the work of the commission included Juan J. Linz, the commission chair, Bolivar Lamounier, Carlos Nino, Carina Perelli, and Arturo Valenzuela. On specific matters, the commission also received the advice of Franz Thedieck, Jugen Roesner, and Delia Ferreira Rubio. This article only makes reference to proposed constitutional provisions dealing with regime type. The Milenio text also called for far-reaching changes in the judicial system through the creation of a council of the judiciary, new norms for decentralization and local government, new definitions of the rights and guarantees of indigenous peoples, and other matters. Many of these suggestions were included in the constitutional reforms adopted in Bolivia in 1993–94—although the provisions dealing with regime type described in this chapter were not adopted. Juan Linz's contribution to the deliberations of the commission was critical, bringing to its work his erudition and encyclopedic knowledge of the constitutional experience of countries in Europe and the Americas. Carlos Nino's contribution was essential particularly to the deliberations involving changes in the judiciary. With his tragic death while attending a meeting of

the commission, Latin America lost one of its most prominent constitutional scholars and a wonderful human being. A text of the proposed constitution can be found in Fundación Milenio, *Proyecto de Reforma a la Constitución Política del Estado 1991–1992*. Serie Instituciones de la democracia (La Paz, Bolivia: Fundación Milenio, 1997).

20. For a description of the politics of coalition building in Bolivian democracy after the establishment of democratic rule, see René Mayorga, "Bolivia's Silent Revolution," *Journal of Democracy* 8, no. 1 (January 1997): 142–56; and Eduardo Gamarra, "Hybrid Presidentialism and Democratization: The Case of Bolivia" in *Presidentialism and Democracy in Latin America*, ed. Scott Mainwaring and Matthew Soberg Shugart (New York: Cambridge University Press, 1997).

CHAPTER 6: THE PREDICAMENT OF SEMI-PRESIDENTIALISM

An earlier version of this paper was originally presented to the Third General Assembly of the Club of Madrid, November 12–13, 2004, and subsequently published as "The Russian Predicament: A Fresh Look at Semi-Presidentialism," *Journal of Democracy* 16, no. 3 (July 2005). We gratefully acknowledge the comments of Raúl Alfonsín, Dante Caputo, Aníbal Cavaco Silva, Jorge Domínguez, Gonzalo Sánchez de Lozada, Hong-Koo Lee, José María Maravall, Jens Meierhenrich, Alfred Stepan, Arturo Valenzuela, and Daniel Zovatto. Any errors remain our own.

1. Giovanni Sartori, for example, suggested that some troubled democracies might benefit from "radically switching to semi-presidentialism"; and Gianfranco Pasquino similarly suggested that "on the whole, under most circumstances, semi-presidential systems appear endowed with both more governmental capabilities and more institutional flexibility than parliamentary and presidential systems." See Sartori, *Comparative Constitutional Engineering: An Inquiry into Structures, Incentives, and Outcomes* (New York: New York University Press, 1994), 137; and Pasquino, "Semi-presidentialism: A Political Model at Work," *European Journal of Political Research* 31, no. 1 (January 1997): 128–37, quotation on 136–37.

2. Lilia Shevtsova, *Yeltsin's Russia: Myths and Reality* (Washington, D.C.: Carnegie Endowment for International Peace, 1999). For monarchic and other aspects of Yeltsin's rule, see Timothy J. Colton, *Yeltsin: A Life* (New York: Basic Books, 2008).

3. Boris Yeltsin, *The View from the Kremlin* (London: HarperCollins, 1994), 6.

4. We will not delve here into the proliferating categories used to encapsulate Russia and many other countries that went through partial democra-

tization during the Third Wave only to regress a few years later. Among the rubrics that have been applied to Russia recently are "managed democracy," "competitive authoritarianism," and the more familiar "delegative democracy." See, for example, Lilia Shevtsova, "Russian Democracy in Eclipse: The Limits of Bureaucratic Authoritarianism," *Journal of Democracy* 15, no. 3 (July 2004): 67–77. Also see Lucan Way and Steven Levitsky, "The Rise of Competitive Authoritarianism," *Journal of Democracy* 13, no. 2 (April 2002).

5. William Maley, "The Shape of the Russian Macroeconomy," in *Russia in Search of Its Future*, ed. Amin Saikal and William Maley (Cambridge: Cambridge University Press, 1995), 48–65, esp. 53.

6. See Stephen White, Richard Rose, and Ian McAllister, *How Russia Votes* (Chatham, N.J.: Chathouse Publishers, 1997), 57–87, esp. 74–76. Also see "Yeltsin Wins Sweeping Powers to Push Reform," *Financial Times* (London), November 2, 1991, 3.

7. Yeltsin avoided submitting the Constitution to a proper referendum, which under Russian law would have needed to be endorsed by 50 percent of the entire electorate. The December 1993 vote, according to Yeltsin's decree, would be valid if turnout was 50 percent, and half of those voting endorsed the initiative. Official figures claimed that turnout for the vote on the Constitution was about 54 percent, but even if this were true, it would mean that Yeltsin's Constitution was actually only approved, and thus legitimized, by 31 percent of all Russian citizens.

8. Cindy Skach, *Borrowing Constitutional Designs: Constitutional Law in Weimar Germany and the French Fifth Republic* (Princeton, N.J.: Princeton University Press, 2005), 15.

9. Clinton Rossiter, *Constitutional Dictatorship: Crisis Government in the Modern Democracies* (Princeton, N.J.: Princeton University Press, 1948). On the relationship between semi-presidentialism and constitutional dictatorship, see Skach, *Borrowing Constitutional Designs*, 12–30, 49–70.

10. See Walter Bagehot, *The English Constitution* (1867; Oxford: Oxford University Press, 2001).

11. Alexander M. Yakovlev, *Striving for Law in a Lawless Land: Memoirs of a Russian Reformer* (London: M. E. Sharpe, 1996), 130. Yakovlev, a legal scholar and former legislator, was a key adviser to the committee that drafted the 1993 Constitution. He later served as presidential plenipotentiary to the Federal Assembly. On fractious tendencies within the legislative branch, see especially Josephine T. Andrews, *When Majorities Fail: The Russian Parliament, 1990–1993* (New York: Cambridge University Press, 2002).

12. On path dependence, see Paul Pierson, *Politics in Time: History, Institutions, and Social Analysis* (Princeton, N.J.: Princeton University Press, 2004).

13. Nor was the rivalry between executive and legislature the only salient

division in the constitutional realm. The balance of power between the federal government and the regions was also hotly contested.

14. Using a modified version of Shugart and Carey's index of presidential power to compare these countries, France's president receives a score of 13, Weimar Germany's president receives a score of 17, and Russia's (1993) president receives a score of 26. In our counting, we have added emergency powers, which Shugart and Carey do not include, but which we feel are crucial. See Mathew Soberg Shugart and John M. Carey, *Presidents and Assemblies: Constitutional Designs and Electoral Dynamics* (Cambridge: Cambridge University Press, 1992), 150–55.

15. See especially M. Steven Fish, *Democracy Derailed in Russia: The Failure of Open Politics* (New York: Cambridge University Press, 2005).

16. On the controversy surrounding such a constitutional choice and the resistance, see Viktor Sheinis, *Moscow News* no. 46 (November 12, 1993).

17. *RFE/RL Research Report*, February 4, 1994.

18. Robert A. Dahl, *Polyarchy: Participation and Opposition* (New Haven, Conn.: Yale University Press, 1971).

19. Before the decision to elongate the presidential term to six years, there was quiet discussion in Moscow of a shift to a parliamentary system. The change was favored by some of the more hard-line and anti-Western associates of Putin, including officials in the security services and the presidential apparatus. One of its appeals was that it would eliminate any kind of fixed term for the country's leader.

20. See the "Conclusions of the Presidency," European Council in Copenhagen Press Release, document DOC/93/3, June 22, 1993, which explicitly spells out the democratic criteria all potential EU members must satisfy before they can be admitted to the EU.

21. Cindy Skach's interview with President Aleksander Kwaśniewski, Warsaw, May 21, 2001.

22. See the discussion of France's current constitutional difficulties, and the critique that its Constitution is "ill adapted to the needs of a modern democracy," in Robert Graham's comment in *Financial Times* (London), September 1, 2004, 15.

CONCLUSION: THE WAY FORWARD

1. Lionel Jospin, *L'Impasse* (Paris: Flammarion, 2007).

Contributors

Felipe Agüero was born in Chile and is the author of *Soldiers, Civilians, and Democracy: Post-Franco Spain in Comparative Perspective* (1995). In its dissertation form, this work was the winner of the Gabriel Almond Award of the American Political Science Association for the best dissertation in comparative politics in 1991–92. He is the co-editor of *Fault Lines of Democracy in Post-transition Latin America* (1998), selected by *Choice* magazine as one of the outstanding academic books of the year, and the Social Science Research Council–supported project *Memorias militares sobre la represión en el Cono Sur: Visiones en disputa en dictadura y democracia* (2005). He is a member of the International Advisory Board of the Global Facilitation Network for Security Sector Reform. Agüero has been a visiting fellow at the Institute for Advanced Study at Princeton and the Kellogg Institute for International Studies at Notre Dame. He is an associate professor of political science at the University of Miami.

Fernando Henrique Cardoso, the president of Brazil from 1995 to 2003, is a scholar who has played key roles in civil society, political society, and the state in his own country and in numerous transnational human rights and democracy movements. In the 1960s Cardoso wrote a book on slavery and capitalism in Brazil. By the early 1970s he held the chair of political science at the University of São Paulo until his teaching rights were revoked by the military regime. In exile in Chile he wrote, with Enzo Faletto, *Dependency and Development in Latin America* (1969). He returned to Brazil to create a public policy institute, CEBRAP, which helped revitalize scholarship and civil society. He increasingly shifted his activities to political society and was a cofounder of the Social Democratic Party of Brazil (PSDB) and leader of this opposition party in the Senate. After serving in the democratic period as foreign minister and finance minister, he was elected president of Brazil. Among his numerous international activities have been his presidency of the International Sociological Association, his occupancy of the Simon Bolivar Chair at Cambridge, and his election as president of the Club of Madrid, an organization of more than fifty former prime ministers and presidents concerned with deepening democracy around the world. He recently published a 700-page reflection on his political life, *A Arte da política: A História que vivi.*

Timothy J. Colton was born in Canada and was a professor of political science at the University of Toronto before moving to Harvard, where he is the Morris and Anna Feldberg Professor of Government and Russian Studies and director of the Davis Center for Russian and Eurasian Studies. He is the former chairman of the Joint Committee on Soviet Studies of the Social Science Research Council and the American Council of Learned Studies and fellow of the Kennan Institute for Advanced Russian Studies. His many books include *Commissars, Commanders, and Civilian Authority: The Structure of Soviet Military Politics; The Dilemma of Reform in the Soviet Union;* and *Moscow: Governing the Soviet Metropolis,* which won the 1985 award for best book in government and political science from the Association of American Publishers. He has written extensively on the problems of super-presidentialism under Yeltsin and delegative democracy under Putin for the *Journal of Democracy; Post-Soviet Affairs; Foreign Affairs;* and the Brookings Foundation; and most extensively in his book *Yeltsin: A Life* (2008).

Narcís Serra holds a PhD in Economics from the University of Barcelona, and after teaching in various Spanish universities was elected mayor of Barcelona in 1979. He served as minister of defense in the socialist government of Felipe González for eight years, some of which time he also served as the vice president of Spain. He is widely considered by democratization specialists to have been the most successful and innovative minister of defense in any of the new democracies in the world. Serra is in wide demand in the European Union and Latin America as an advisor on strategies of democratic reforms concerning human security. From 1986 to 2004 Serra was a member of the Spanish Parliament from Barcelona. He helped found the Barcelona Institute of International Studies

(IBEI) and was a key intellectual organizer of the Club of Madrid's 2005 International Summit on Democracies and Terrorism. Among his many publications are, edited with Manuel Castells, *Europa en construcción: Integración, identitades y seguridad* (2004); *La transición military: Reflexiones en torno a la reforma democrática de las fuerzas armadas* (2008); and a volume edited with Joseph Stiglitz, *The Washington Consensus Reconsidered: Toward a New Global Governance* (2008).

Richard Simeon, both as an academic and a policy participant, has been intensively involved with federal relations in Canada for over three decades. He is a professor of political science and law at the University of Toronto and has been the William Lyon Mackenzie Professor of Canadian Studies at Harvard University. He is the author of *Federal-Provincial Diplomacy: The Making of Recent Policy in Canada* (1972), which won the Matha Derthick Book Award of the American Political Science Association in 2005 for its "lasting contribution to the study of federalism." His many other books include *Is Partnership Possible?* (1998); *Citizen Engagement in Conflict Resolution* (with Janice Gross Stein and David R. Cameron, 1997); and *Toward a Social Contract* (1994). Simeon has been director of the School of Public Administration, Queens University, Canada. He has served on many public policy committees concerning issues such as constitutional redesign, new patterns of federalism, and democratic renewal and frequently gives witness to the Parliament of Canada. He is a fellow of the Royal Society of Canada.

Cindy Skach is professor of comparative government and law at the University of Oxford and a fellow and tutor at Brasenose College. She previously was an associate professor of government at Harvard University and faculty associate of the Minda de Gunzburg Center for European Studies and the Davis Center for Russian Studies at Harvard. Her D.Phil., St. Antony's College, the University of Oxford, on semi-presidentialism won the Georges Lavau Award of the American Political Science Association for the best dissertation on France written during 2000–2005. She was a postdoctoral fellow at the Harriman Institute for the Advanced Study of Russia at Columbia University. She is the author of *Borrowing Constitutional Designs: Constitutional Law in Weimar Germany and the French Fifth Republic* (2005) and the forthcoming *The Constitution of Peoples*.

Her articles have appeared in such journals as *World Politics*; *Journal of Democracy*; *Journal of Common Market Studies*; *American Journal of International Law*; and the *International Journal of Constitutional Law.*

Alfred Stepan is the author of numerous books, including *The Military in Politics: Changing Patterns in Brazil* (1971); *State and Society: Peru in Comparative Perspective* (1978); *The Breakdown of Democratic Regimes*, (edited with Juan Linz, 1978); *Problems of Democratic Transition and Consolidation: Southern Europe, South America, and Post-communist Europe* (with Juan Linz, 1996); *Arguing Comparative Politics* (2001); and *Democracy in Multinational Societies: India and other Polities* (with Juan Linz and Yogendra Yadav, forthcoming). He is the Wallace Sayre Professor of Government and director of the Center for Democracy, Toleration, and Religion at Columbia University. Stepan was previously a fellow of All Souls College and Gladstone Professor of Government at the University of Oxford and the first rector and president of Central European University in Budapest, Warsaw, and Prague. He is a fellow of the American Academy of Arts and Sciences and of the British Academy. He began his career as a special correspondent for *The Economist.*

Arturo Valenzuela is the author of the classic *The Breakdown of Democratic Regimes: Chile* (1978), as well as numerous other works, including *The Failure of Presidential Democracy*, a two-volume book he edited with Juan Linz (1994); and *Hacia una democracia moderna: La opción democratica* (with Juan Linz and Arend Lijphart, 1990). He is a professor of government and director of the Center for Latin American Studies at Georgetown University. He previously taught at Duke University. During President Clinton's second term, Valenzuela served at the White House as special assistant to the president and senior director for Inter-American Affairs at the National Security Council. He is frequently heard on the BBC and NPR and appears on such programs as the *NewsHour with Jim Lehrer*, *Nightline*, and the *Today Show.* His political commentary has been published by the *Washington Post* and thirty other newspapers.

Ashutosh Varshney is a professor of political science at Brown University. He received his PhD from MIT in 1990 and taught at Harvard University and the University of Michigan, Ann Arbor, before joining Brown. In 2008, he won the Guggenheim and Carnagie awards for his research. His books include *Ethnic Conflict and Civic Life: Hindus and Muslims in India* (2002), which won the Gregory Luebbert Prize of the American Political Science Association; *Democracy, Development, and the Countryside: Urban-Rural Struggles in India* (1995), which won the Daniel Lerner prize at MIT; *India in the Era of Economic Reforms* (with Jeffrey Sachs, 2000); and *Midnight's Diaspora: Critical Encounters with Salman Rushdie* (with Daniel Herwitz, 2009).

Index